Editor
Brent L. Fox, M. Ed.

Editor in Chief
Karen J. Goldfluss, M.S. Ed.

Creative Director
Sarah M. Fournier

Cover Artist
Sarah Kim

Illustrator
Clint McKnight

Art Coordinator
Renée Mc Elwee

Imaging
Amanda R. Harter

Publisher
Mary D. Smith, M.S. Ed.

GRADE 4

LET'S GET THIS DAY STARTED
Reading

TCR 8126

- Start the day off right with engaging reading and writing activities
- 85 high-interest fiction and non-fiction passages organized by theme
- Reading passages include standards-based questions reinforcing essential comprehension skills
- Culminating writing activity in each unit encourages students to revisit multiple reading passages

Teacher Created Resources

Author
Ruth Foster, M. Ed.

CORRELATED TO COMMON CORE STANDARDS

For correlations to the Common Core State Standards, visit *http://www.teachercreated.com/standards/*.

Teacher Created Resources
12621 Western Avenue
Garden Grove, CA 92841
www.teachercreated.com

ISBN: 978-1-4206-8126-0

© 2018 Teacher Created Resources
Made in U.S.A.

Teacher Created Resources

Table of Contents

Table of Contents (cont.)

Introduction

Reading should be something that students look forward to. However, sometimes students must find fun and accessible literature *before* they can realize how enjoyable reading can be! The passages in this book contain high-interest topics that will immediately hook even the most stubborn of readers. Fun themes, surprise twists, and grade-appropriate content will motivate and excite young readers. Additionally, the passages in this book were designed to be accessible to students of varying reading abilities. Basic sight words are introduced and then reinforced with repetition and practice. As new words are introduced, they are repeated and written into the story in ways that allow a student to use context clues to decipher their meanings.

Each unit begins with five reading passages. The first several passages are short and include four multiple-choice questions. The remaining passages are a bit longer and have five multiple-choice questions. The passages in each unit are a mixture of fact and fiction. The last page of the unit calls for a written response to a prompt that incorporates the theme of the unit.

The passages in each unit are all linked by a loose theme. As the students continue to read more of the unit, they will begin to discover the common thread that weaves together each collection of stories. This approach broadens a student's comprehension and understanding of the subject matter. It allows students to practice new words in various stories and in different genres. It also shows students how separate passages can be linked with other passages and used collectively to expand one's horizons and views. This approach ultimately allows students to become familiar with the flexibility of word use, different viewpoints, and how we can learn from both fiction and nonfiction texts.

All of the texts and activities in the *Let's Get This Day Started* series have been aligned to the Common Core State Standards (CCSS). Visit *http://www.teachercreated.com/standards/* for all standards correlations.

Using the Book

Teachers should not feel restricted by a daily warm-up activity. Sometimes, schedules change. A morning assembly, a make-up lesson, or just an extra-busy day can easily throw off the classroom schedule for days. A teacher never knows what his or her week is going to look like. *Let's Get This Day Started* does not need to be completed every day or even every other day. Teachers can take their time and arrange the activities to fit their own schedules. The book is written so the teacher can stop wherever and whenever he or she wants. A teacher may choose to do a unit a week (one passage a day), or at other times, spread a unit out over a few weeks. There is no right or wrong way.

At the beginning of the year, a teacher may choose to have the class read the passages together as a group before asking them to read each passage again on their own. A teacher may also choose to have students reread passages several weeks later to practice fluidity or so that the students can see how "easy" the passages have become.

The multiple-choice questions in *Let's Get This Day Started* assess all levels of comprehension—from recall to critical thinking. The questions are based on fundamental reading skills found in scope-and-sequence charts across the nation. Examples of just some of the question styles used in this series include:

- recalling information
- sequencing in chronological order
- using prior knowledge
- identifying synonyms and antonyms
- visualizing
- knowing and using grade-level vocabulary

- recognizing the main idea
- using context clues to understand new words
- identifying supporting details
- making inferences
- understanding cause and effect
- drawing conclusions

All question stems and answers are written so that they are a continuation of reading practice and critical thinking. If an answer choice includes an unfamiliar word, the correct answer can still be found by the process of elimination. Remind students to read every answer choice! If the answer doesn't jump out at them, they can get it right by crossing out the wrong answers first.

The written response (Write On!) pages require students to look back at the passages they have read in each unit for facts, ideas, or vocabulary. Students are encouraged to respond creatively to a variety of fun writing prompts and then support their answers by referring back to examples from several of the reading passages.

Use the Tracking Sheet on page 108 to keep track of which passages you have given to your students, or distribute copies of the sheet for students to monitor their own progress.

Name: _maleha fonseca vega_

What the Droop Means

You see two camels—one with a hump that isn't drooping and one with a hump that is leaning over. Why is there a difference?

Camels, also known as "ships of the desert," can go for a week or more without water. They can go several months without food. When food is scarce, camels live off the fat reserves stored in their humps. The camel with the drooping hump is not sick. It has just used up its fat reserves. Its hump will regain its shape once the camel is fed and watered.

When you're really thirsty, you can drink a few glasses of water. Compare that to a camel that can drink up to 32 gallons of water during one drinking session! Compare yourself to a 100-pound camel. If you lost 40 pounds, you would die, but a camel can safely lose 40 percent of its weight before needing to eat again.

1. When something is *saved* or *put away for future use*, it is
   a. scarce. **b.** shaped. **c.** reserved. **d.** regained.

2. A camel has a hump that is not drooping. Most likely, this means that
   a. the camel has been well-watered and fed.
   b. it has just walked for days across a hot desert.
   c. it is thirsty enough to drink 32 gallons in one session.
   d. the camel lives in the rainforest.

3. This text is mainly about
   a. animals of the desert.
   b. what camels eat.
   c. how much water a camel needs.
   d. what a camel's hump shows.

4. One reason camels are known as "ships of the desert" may be because
   a. camels have been used to carry parts of ships.
   b. camels have been used to carry things across deserts.
   c. camels swim through sand.
   d. camels drink a lot of water, and ships sail in water.

Name: _maleha_

Desert Survival

The assignment was to share a desert survival tip or adaptation. Rory said, "The thorny devil has a mind-boggling adaptation. If you get rained on, you can only drink the water that falls into your mouth. Not so for this Australian lizard. It has tiny grooves all over its body. To get drinking water, it walks through dew-covered grass or shrubs. Then, it gulps. As it gulps, no matter where the water is on its body, the water travels through the grooves and into its mouth!"

Ava said, "Fennec foxes are the smallest foxes, but they have the biggest ears. They live in the African Sahara Desert. Their huge ears help them stay cool because they are used to dissipate heat."

Luis went next. He stood and spoke in a firm and unwavering voice, "I have a survival tip rather than an adaptation. Circle rather than enter deserts!"

1. In what position or state would you dissipate the most heat?
   a. holding out your bare arms
   b. curled up into a ball
   c. hugging your arms to your chest
   d. wearing a hat and mittens

2. What did Luis mean when he shared his survival tip with the class?
   a. Draw a line around all deserts.
   b. Be firm when it comes to entering the desert.
   c. Rather than go through a desert, go around it.
   d. You don't need to adapt if you want to survive.

3. Why might the teacher think Luis didn't do his homework?
   a. Luis spoke in a firm and unwavering voice.
   b. Rory's facts weren't commonly known.
   c. Luis didn't have to read anything to come up with his tip.
   d. Ava had to look up information for her answer.

4. When something is *mind boggling*, it is
   a. frightening.   b. ordinary.   c. unknown.   d. astonishing.

Name: _____

Surviving the Gorge

The Colorado River was flowing through the desert gorge. Approximately 1,500 feet above the dry, rocky walls, a two-inch wire stretched a quarter of a mile. It went from one rim of the canyon to the other. There was no safety net below the wire, but a man without a safety harness was walking across it.

The man's name was Nic Wallender. Nic carried a 45-pound bar to help him keep his balance, but his 23-minute walk was fraught with danger. He was buffeted with winds ranging from a safe 18 miles per hour to a treacherous 30 miles per hour. Two times he had to kneel on the wire and wait out the strongest gusts.

Nic practiced on his parents' practice wire when he was little. The wire was only two feet off the ground. Nic's parents would throw objects at Nic while he was practicing. They were not being cruel. They were teaching him not to be distracted. They knew that later, if Nic didn't focus, he could fall and die. He had to learn to let nothing interfere with his concentration.

1. When a person is *buffeted*, he or she is
   a. squeezed or hugged.
   b. viewed or seen.
   c. pounded or rocked.
   d. tired or weary.

2. This text is mainly about
   a. a desert walk.
   b. a high-wire act in the desert.
   c. wind speeds in the desert.
   d. a dry, rocky gorge.

3. Most likely, when Nic was kneeling on the wire,
   a. he focused only on completing the walk.
   b. he was thinking about his childhood.
   c. he was hoping his parents would throw something at him.
   d. he was taking the time to relax and rest.

4. How long was Nic on the wire?
   a. 23 minutes   b. 24 minutes   c. 30 minutes   d. 35 minutes

Name: _Malena_

No Eyelids

The Palmato gecko lives in the Namib Desert. This desert is one of the oldest deserts on Earth. It is filled with some of the world's highest sand dunes. The dunes range in color from orange to red. The red hues are due to the high amount of iron in the sand.

The gecko has webbed feet. Its webbed feet are similar to snowshoes. Snowshoes stop the wearer from sinking into soft snow. The gecko's webbed feet allow the lizard to run on loose sand and not sink in. The webbing also helps the nocturnal gecko burrow under the sand, so it can sleep during the hot days.

The Palmato gecko has no eyelids. It keeps its eyes clean by licking them with its long tongue. There are times when the gecko licks its eyes for other reasons. What reason could it be? The Namib Desert runs along the Atlantic coast of Namibia. Sometimes, ocean fog will blow onto the dunes. When fog condenses, it changes from a gas to a liquid. When warm fog hits the gecko's cold eyes, it condenses. The water vapor changes to liquid. To quench its thirst, the gecko licks water droplets off its own eyes!

1. How is a gecko's foot similar to a snowshoe?
   a. They look the same.
   b. They are both used for burrowing.
   c. They help one to sink.
   d. They have the same purpose.

2. When something is *quenched*, it is
   a. satisfied.   b. ancient.   c. nocturnal.   d. pleased.

3. From the text, you can tell that *water vapor* is
   a. a liquid.   b. a gas.   c. a solid.   d. a droplet.

4. What sentence best sums up the text?
   a. The Namib Desert is one of the oldest deserts in the world.
   b. Geckos are amazing lizards.
   c. A gecko's body allows it to live in the Namib Desert.
   d. Dunes that are rich in iron have red hues.

5. Most likely, why is the Palmato gecko nocturnal?
   a. It is less likely to slip on the dunes at night.
   b. It can escape the high daytime temperatures.
   c. It feeds on insects that are more active when the desert is light.
   d. It has a very long tongue.

Name: _____

The New Colony

Tarn said, "I can't believe how hot it is here! It's a lot hotter than what we're used to, but I think we can adapt. We already know how to deal with the lack of water, and all the red rocks and sandy soil remind me of home. I think this is the best location we're going to find for establishing a new settlement colony."

"I suppose that we can burrow underground and set up our living headquarters there," Lexta said pensively. "Temperatures plummet at night, so we can just set up a schedule where we're basically nocturnal. We can get all the outside work done after the sun has set."

"Time to stop talking," Rella said. "Let's act!" With Rella urging them on, Tarn and Lexta put on their suits and went outside. They meant to run, but instead they staggered. They could barely move. "I should have known," Rella said. "There is less gravity on Mars because it is a smaller planet. There, we only weighed 38 pounds. Here on Earth, we weigh a whopping 100 pounds! We may not be able to stay here. Earth's gravity is too much! It makes the planet inhospitable!"

1. When something is *unwelcoming* or *uninviting*, it
   - **a.** can barely move.
   - **b.** is inhospitable.
   - **c.** reminds one of home.
   - **d.** is basically nocturnal.

2. Where does the reader find out where Tarn, Lexta, and Rella are from?
   - **a.** in the title
   - **b.** in the first paragraph
   - **c.** in the second paragraph
   - **d.** in the third paragraph

3. Why did the author pick this time to let the reader know?
   - **a.** She wanted you to think rather than act.
   - **b.** She wanted you to feel surprised.
   - **c.** She wanted you to learn temperature facts.
   - **d.** She wanted you to understand why many animals are nocturnal.

4. Why did Tarn, Lexta, and Rella stagger?
   - **a.** Their extra weight made it hard for them to walk.
   - **b.** It was too hot to run.
   - **c.** They didn't have enough water.
   - **d.** They kept slipping on the sandy and rocky soil.

5. From the text, you can tell that
   - **a.** Earth was settled by aliens from Mars.
   - **b.** Day and night time temperatures in deserts are constant.
   - **c.** Nothing can live in the desert.
   - **d.** The force of gravity is affected by planet size.

Name: _____

Write On!

Write about three of the animals mentioned in this unit. Explain what it is about them that helps them to survive in the desert.

_____

_____

_____

_____

_____

_____

_____

_____

_____

_____

_____

_____

_____

_____

_____

_____

_____

_____

_____

_____

_____

Name: _____

Unforeseen Problem

Stuntmen and stuntwomen are in almost every movie you see. You may think that you're seeing your favorite actor or actress jump out of a moving car or an airplane, but it is most often the stunt person. The stunt person gets paid to do all the dangerous work. The stunt person puts on wigs and clothes to look like the actor. Then the stunt person acts for the actor!

In a recent movie about World War II, one stuntman had to pretend to be dead. His job was to lie down in dirty water and let rats crawl over his face. To make the scene more realistic, maggots were spread all over his "decaying corpse."

An unforeseen problem came up when the maggots were strewn over his body and the rats were let loose. What was the unexpected problem? The rats ate the maggots! The director said, "They were slurping them up."

1. Another title for this text might be
    a. "What a Rat Eats."
    b. "Why Some People Choose Stunt Work."
    c. "The Dangers of Acting."
    d. "Stunt Work."

2. From the text, you can tell that stuntmen and stuntwomen
    a. often shake with fear.
    b. are very shy.
    c. get tired of doing all the dangerous work.
    d. are very daring.

3. When something *decays*, it
    a. stays still.   b. rots.   c. is strewn.   d. crawls.

4. Which is most likely to be an unforeseen event?
    a. a meteor falling through your roof while you're eating
    b. getting a flat tire when you ride over broken glass
    c. feeling thirsty after running two miles on a hot day
    d. falling asleep at your desk after staying up too late

Name: _____

A Brave Actor

Brian said, "My favorite actor is Daniel Stern. He played the burglar Marv in the movie *Home Alone*. I like him because he never used a stunt double. He was the one who stepped on all those glass ornaments and that huge nail. In the scene with the tarantula on his face, it was really him! Now, that's a really brave actor!"

Darrell said, "I don't want to burst your bubble, but when Marv stepped on that rubber nail, the scene was filmed with a rubber foot. He did step on all the ornaments with his bare feet, but the ornaments were made out of candy. As for the tarantula scene, he only agreed to have the spider on his face for one take. He had to mime screaming during filming because otherwise the sound would have scared the tarantula. He screamed later, and the sound was dubbed in."

1. This text is
   a. fiction but fact-filled.
   b. historical fact.
   c. nonfiction and factual.
   d. science fiction.

2. How was it possible for Stern to step on ornaments with his bare feet?
   a. He wore rubber feet.
   b. He was really brave.
   c. The ornaments were made from candy.
   d. He only mimed stepping on them.

3. What did Darrell mean when he said he didn't want to "burst his bubble"?
   a. He didn't want to pop Brian's bubble.
   b. He didn't want Brian to mime blowing bubbles.
   c. He didn't want to scream when he found out the truth.
   d. He didn't want Brian to feel disappointed.

4. Why might Brian still consider Stern to be a brave man?
   a. He was willing to play a foolish burglar.
   b. He allowed the tarantula to be put on his face.
   c. He stepped on a rubber nail.
   d. He only used a stunt double for dubbing.

Name: _____

Director's Choice

Directors have to make choices. Who will they choose to act in their movies? Where will they film them? Will they construct sets, film on location, or use computer generated imagery (CGI)?

Tim Burton was the director of the film *Charlie and the Chocolate Factory.* He filmed a scene with 40 squirrels cracking nuts. For that scene, Burton didn't want to rely on CGI. He hired trainers. They began working ten weeks before filming. First, they bottle-fed newborn squirrels. This created a bond. Then, they taught the squirrels what to do. Burton ended up having to supplement his footage with CGI, but he said that "for the close-ups and the main action, they're the real thing."

There is also a scene in the movie in which Charlie floats down a chocolate river. At first, CGI was going to be used to make the river. Instead, over 200,000 gallons of fake chocolate was used. Nine different shades of chocolate were tested. Burton then chose the hue he liked best for his chocolate river.

1. Why did the trainers bottle-feed the squirrels?
   a. They didn't want the squirrels to be hungry.
   b. They needed to save the nuts for the movie.
   c. They felt that it was better for the main action.
   d. They wanted the squirrels to feel close to them.

2. What is most likely CGI?
   a. a flying dinosaur
   b. a sleeping cheetah
   c. a girl playing the piano
   d. a dolphin swimming

3. A *hue* is a
   a. color or shade.
   b. film or movie.
   c. set or location.
   d. choice or option.

4. From the text, you can tell that
   a. directors are more important that actors or actresses.
   b. most directors prefer CGI over live animals.
   c. directors need to start planning a long time before filming.
   d. live footage cannot be supplemented with CGI.

Name: _____

Snake's-Eye View

Alan Root was a documentary filmmaker. He filmed animals in innovative ways. In one instance, he concealed cameras under turtle shells! This allowed for, as Root described it, a snake's-eye view close-up. Root was filming the migration of the wildebeest. The cameras allowed him to get amazing images of the thundering hooves.

Root was also the first man to film animals by using hot-air balloons. Cars and jeeps were loud. They couldn't go over rocky or dangerous ground. Planes went too fast. Helicopters were slower, but they made too much noise. Balloons were quiet. They drifted slowly. Animals were often unaware that they were being filmed.

One time, Root took pictures of a spitting cobra. This snake aims its venom at the eye of its prey. It spits with deadly accuracy. Root used his wife as the target. She put on big plastic glasses. She approached. She had to be close enough that the snake didn't lose interest. She had to be far enough away that she wasn't bitten. Over and over, the snake sprayed her glasses. Over and over, Root's wife would wipe off the spray and move closer for another take.

1. This text is mainly about
   a. animal movies.
   b. a documentary filmmaker.
   c. using hot-air balloons.
   d. how snakes view the world.

2. When something is done in an *innovative* way, it is
   a. concealed.
   b. done so that one is unaware.
   c. accurate.
   d. done in a new or pioneering way.

3. What would happen if Root's wife got too close to the cobra?
   a. It would spit venom on her.
   b. It would approach her.
   c. It would bite her.
   d. It would lose interest.

4. What might Root use for filming today that he couldn't use before?
   a. motorcycles   b. rocket ships   c. drones   d. helicopters

5. From the text, you can tell that Root
   a. never had an accident in a hot-air balloon.
   b. found it easier to film wild animals than people.
   c. believed that the best pictures were taken at ground level.
   d. know something about animal behavior before he started filming.

Name: _____

Whale Watching

Laura had always wanted to see a whale. She knew that, from mid-December to mid-March, more than 25,000 gray whales migrate from Alaska to Mexico. Laura timed her visit to California so she could see the whales spouting and breaching as they swam south.

Laura walked to a bluff. She just knew that this was the day that she would see a whale. Looking down, she saw the sparkling blue water. She saw one big boat and a few small boats bobbing about. Suddenly she saw something slicing through the water. It was a huge fin! Laura watched in horror as the triangular shape came closer. Then all Laura could see was a huge gaping mouth, filled with rows of sharp, jagged teeth! Laura's heart leapt into her mouth as she saw the jaws snap shut. With a terrible splintering sound, the boat broke in two. When Laura saw a man flailing and thrashing about in the water, she closed her eyes. She didn't want to see what was going to happen next.

Then Laura heard something. It was a man on the big boat yelling through a bullhorn. "Cut!" he cried. "That scene was perfect!"

1. Who was the man speaking through the bullhorn?
   a. a whale scientist
   b. a fishing captain
   c. a movie director
   d. a boat engineer

2. If a man is waving and flapping his arms, he is
   a. flailing them.
   b. splintering them.
   c. breaching them.
   d. slicing them.

3. In what order does the author want you to feel the following emotions?
   a. terror, calm interest, relief, surprise
   b. relief, surprise, calm interest, terror
   c. calm interest, terror, surprise, relief
   d. surprise, terror, relief, calm interest

4. What did the author mean when she wrote "Laura's heart leapt into her mouth"?
   a. Laura's heart jumped into her mouth.
   b. Laura leapt up.
   c. Laura almost fell off the bluff.
   d. Laura was very nervous.

5. Laura could have been in California on
   a. December 1.   b. February 4.   c. April 15.   d. September 23.

Name: _____

Write On!

Describe the animal actors that are mentioned in this unit. Were they CGI? Use evidence from the texts in your answer.

Then, tell why you think the directors chose to film with CGI or with live animals.

Finally, explain whether you think Alan Root's movie would have been a real documentary if he had used CGI for the spitting cobra. Explain your answer and support it with evidence from the text.

_____

_____

_____

_____

_____

_____

_____

_____

_____

_____

_____

_____

_____

_____

_____

_____

_____

_____

_____

_____

_____

Name: _____

Just as Horrible

Ask a person to name an animal that defends itself with a foul-smelling odor. Most people will tell you a skunk. Very few people will think of an albatross.

Albatrosses are seabirds. In the bird world, they are the kings of soaring. They are built like gliders, with long, narrow wings. They can soar for hours and travel hundreds of miles without flapping their wings once! Albatrosses are rarely seen on land. They remain at sea, gliding through the air and sleeping on the water until they are ready to breed and raise a chick.

Albatrosses raise their young on remote islands. There are fewer predators on far-away islands, but there are times when albatrosses still need to defend themselves. How do they do this? When an albatross feels threatened, it will spit out bad-smelling oil from its stomach. The smell is atrocious. It is so horrible that it will drive any intruder away.

1. Most likely, how many chicks does an adult albatross raise each breeding season?
   a. one   b. two   c. three   d. four

2. Why can the planet Saturn be described as *remote*?
   a. It has rings.
   b. It is blue.
   c. It is so far away.
   d. It is rarely seen.

3. Most likely, what kind of predator might an albatross have to protect itself from when on its nest?
   a. a shark
   b. a house cat
   c. a moose
   d. another kind of sea bird

4. What is not true about albatrosses?
   a. They can soar for hours.
   b. They have wings that are as wide as they are long.
   c. They are rarely seen on land.
   d. They can travel hundreds of miles without flapping their wings.

Name: _____

Deadly Spit

Everyone knows about spitting cobras, but they're not so impressive. Their spit is venomous, so, of course, they can use it to blind their enemies or drive them away. I don't need venom or any other kind of poison. I'm much more impressive because I hunt by spitting plain water.

Even if my dinner is ten feet away, I'm able to hit it and bring it down with my first shot. Of course, I had to practice to be this accurate. What happens if I miss? I'm persistent. I don't give up. If I have to make multiple tries, I will.

It is true that sharks are mighty hunters, but they have sharp, jagged teeth to hunt with. I place my lips so that they just break the surface of the water. Then, I contract my gill covers in order to force water through my mouth. I am the mighty and magnificent water-spitting hunter! I am the archerfish!

1. A proverb is a wise saying. What proverb would the archerfish most likely agree with?
   a. Better to be safe than sorry.
   b. Lost time is never found again.
   c. If at first you don't succeed, try, try again.
   d. Out of sight, out of mind.

2. Why does the archerfish feel it is better than a spitting cobra?
   a. The archerfish does not spit venom.
   b. The archerfish can blind its prey.
   c. The archerfish is accurate.
   d. The archerfish can contract its gill covers.

3. This text is told from the viewpoint of a
   a. fish who thinks it is very impressive.
   b. hunter who has sharp, jagged teeth.
   c. fish who is not persistent.
   d. hunter who can defend itself from sharks.

4. Most likely, the archerfish eats
   a. little fish that swim under the water.
   b. dead insects or bugs floating on the water.
   c. insects or bugs that are alive and above the water.
   d. seaweed and other water plants.

Name: _____

Six Questions

1. Is it extinct?

   No, it isn't extinct, and it presently lives in an aquatic environment.

2. Does its aquatic environment consist of salt or fresh water?

   Its habitat is salt water.

3. If you had to compare it to a fictional character, whom would you say it is most like?

   It is most akin to Winnie the Pooh. Winnie the Pooh was a bear who ate so much at his friend Rabbit's house that he couldn't fit out the door when it was time to go home. This animal will burrow into a dead carcass when it falls to the ocean floor. Sometimes, it eats so much it can't get out! It has to wait until it digests its meal.

4. Does it have a heart?

   Yes, it has multiple hearts. It has three, in fact.

5. How does it get oxygen if it is burrowed inside a carcass?

   Its hearts can beat for hours without oxygen. It is believed that they are powered by fats stored inside its body.

6. Are you making this up?

   Look up the "hagfish," and you can verify everything I said.

1. Where are you most likely to find a hagfish?
   - **a.** the bottom of a lake
   - **b.** near the ocean bottom
   - **c.** at the mouth of a river
   - **d.** in small mountain ponds

2. How many hearts does a hagfish have?
   - **a.** zero
   - **b.** one
   - **c.** two
   - **d.** three

3. When you *verify* something, you
   - **a.** burrow into it.
   - **b.** check that it is true.
   - **c.** are akin to it.
   - **d.** power it with stored fat.

4. At times, why does the hagfish have to remain where it is after eating?
   - **a.** Parts of its body are too big to fit through the hole it dug.
   - **b.** It does not have enough oxygen to keep moving.
   - **c.** It has to wait for the aquatic environment to dry up.
   - **d.** It remains safe from bears that are catching fish.

Name: _____

Not All!

Many people believe that all male deer have antlers. While it's true that only bucks have antlers, many species of deer don't have antlers at all. There are about 40 species of deer, and not all of the bucks have antlers.

Deer live in all different kinds of habitats. The ones that live in tropical environments are the smaller ones. If they do have antlers, the antlers are very small. With a little bit of pondering, one can come up with a good explanation as to why. There is a lot of vegetation in tropical places. It would be hard to run through a leafy jungle if your antlers kept getting caught on vines and branches!

Bigger deer can live where it is cold. Their big bodies can hold heat for a long time. Sometimes, they can even get too hot! When this happens, warm blood rushes to their antlers. There, the blood quickly cools down because it is closer to the outside air. One should remember that antlers are not horns. Horns are permanently attached to the skull. Antlers break off every year at the skull, and new ones grow in their place.

1. You see a deer with huge antlers. Most likely, you are
   a. in a tropical jungle with lots of plants.
   b. in a hot forest filled with tangled vines.
   c. in a shady jungle thick with leaves and branches.
   d. on a grassy plain where it snows in the winter.

2. When you *ponder* something, you
   a. cool it down.   **c.** remember it.
   b. think about it.   **d.** break it.

3. Moose are a kind of deer. How many species of deer are there?
   a. There are exactly 10 more kinds.   **c.** There are about 40 more kinds.
   b. There are almost 20 more kinds.   **d.** There are more than 60 more kinds.

4. How does a horn differ from an antler?
   a. Horns break off at the skull.
   b. Horns are used to cool blood.
   c. Horns grow back every year.
   d. Horns are permanently attached to the skull.

5. What statement is correct?
   a. No female deer have antlers.   **c.** Most small deer have antlers.
   b. All male deer have antlers.   **d.** No large deer have antlers.

Name: _____

Frustrated and Weary!

I'm fed up and tired! Why am I so frustrated and weary? Everyone thinks that spiders only spin silk to make webs. It's about time they learned differently. I'm a bola spider, and although I spin silk, I do not make webs. What I do with my silk is much more interesting and, I think, remarkable.

What I do first is spin a ball of sticky silk that I attach to the end of a strong thread. Then, I attract male moths by imitating the smell of a female moth. When the unsuspecting male comes close, I hold on to the end of the thread and swing my ball out like a fisherman! When I make contact, the moth can't get away! It sticks to the sticky ball as I pull in my line.

Although all spiders spin silk for their egg sacs, not all of us use it for catching prey. Jumping spiders also don't need it because they are such fantastic hunters. Jumping spiders can leap more than 50 times their body length! That feat is equivalent to you jumping from one end of a football field to the other in a single bound!

1. If an animal is *unsuspecting*,
   a. it can't spin silk.
   b. it can catch prey.
   c. it doesn't know what is about to happen.
   d. it is frustrated and weary.

2. Why did the author say you could jump "from one end of a football field to another in a single bound"?
   a. so that you could picture how great the distance is a spider can jump—even if it is a short distance for you
   b. so that you could understand why some spiders only spin silk for their egg sacks
   c. so that you could begin to see that jumping spiders are better than spiders that build webs
   d. so that you could see how much more remarkable a spider is than you

3. To catch its dinner, what does the bola spider have to do besides spin silk?
   a. jump 50 times its body length
   b. spin an egg sack
   c. make a web
   d. imitate the smell of a female moth

4. The next paragraph of this text would most likely be about
   a. a spider that can dive under water to catch its prey.
   b. how many eyes a spider has.
   c. why a spider is not an insect.
   d. the largest spider.

5. This text is mainly about
   a. frustrated and weary spiders.
   b. what a bola spider thinks and can do.
   c. how spiders use silk for their egg sacks.
   d. why some spiders are more remarkable than others.

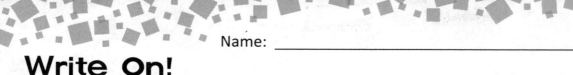

Name: _____

Write On!

In this unit, you read about five different kinds of animals. Choose any of the animals except for the hagfish. Then, write six questions and answers about the animal you chose.

Use the "Six Questions" text as a general guide. You can use the same exact wording, or you can use different questions.

You **must** discuss the animal's habitat or environment and compare it to a fictional character.

1. Question: _____

   Answer: _____

   _____

2. Question: _____

   Answer: _____

   _____

3. Question: _____

   Answer: _____

   _____

4. Question: _____

   Answer: _____

   _____

5. Question: _____

   Answer: _____

   _____

6. Question: _____

   Answer: _____

   _____

Name: _____

Man-Eating Piranhas

Sports writer Bob Peel reported on an "accidental mix-up." The mix-up occurred at a fish hatchery. The article came out on April 1, 1974. Peel wrote that several dozen piranhas had been accidentally released. They had gotten mixed in with some trout. The piranhas were dangerous. They could "completely devour an ox in less than five minutes."

Peel warned anglers to stay out of the water. When fishing, they needed to stay at least three feet away from the banks of streams. Even the water in the fountain at the downtown courthouse was unsafe!

A television news reporter read the story. He repeated the warning on the news. Terror spread. People were calling Peel in a panic. Peel told people it had all been a prank. It was a joke for April Fool's Day. The television reporter should have read the whole story. The last line said, "This is baloney. ALL PURE BALONEY."

1. From the text, you can tell that an *angler* is another word for
   a. a person who reads the sports section of a newspaper.
   b. a person who works at a fish hatchery.
   c. a person who listens to the news on television.
   d. a person who fishes with a rod and a line.

2. What can you learn from this text?
   a. Some news may be based on incomplete information.
   b. All news is false and made up.
   c. What you read is always true.
   d. You do not need to read carefully when checking facts.

3. Most likely, how did Peel feel once he started getting phone calls?
   a. terrified   b. hungry   c. surprised   d. unsafe

4. When something is *devoured*, it is
   a. wolfed down and eaten.
   b. tasted and then sipped.
   c. nibbled and then spit out.
   d. eaten slowly over time.

Name: _____

Nessie

Grant's mother asked Grant where he had disappeared to. When Grant replied, "I went to visit Nessie," his mother stiffened.

"Grant," she said sternly, "Nessie is not real. There is no such thing as the Loch Ness monster. It has been proven that the photographs were fakes. The entire story was invented for tourists. It's nothing but a sham. Scientists have even probed the bottom of the lake. Her existence cannot be verified. She is only a figment of your imagination."

When Grant started to protest, his mother raised a warning finger. "One more word," she admonished him, "and you'll be sent to your room."

That evening, Grant sat on the pier that extended out over the water. He waited patiently until he saw a large shadow moving underneath the water. When the huge head of the long-necked monster poked out, Grant gave it a hug. "You're my best friend," he said.

1. When something is *verified*, it is
    a. a figment of your imagination.
    b. checked and proven to be true.
    c. a fake and a sham.
    d. extended out over the water.

2. Most likely, people would say they saw the Loch Ness monster because
    a. they spotted it at the bottom of the lake.
    b. they have no imagination.
    c. it came up and hugged them while they were sitting at the end of a pier.
    d. they want tourists to come to the lake and spend money while looking for the monster.

3. Most likely, Grant is
    a. old.
    b. afraid.
    c. lonely.
    d. strange.

4. What did Grant's mother say when she scolded him?
    a. "Nessie is not real."
    b. "One more word, and you'll be sent to your room."
    c. "It's nothing but a sham."
    d. "Scientists have probed the bottom of the lake."

Name: _____

Optical Illusion

Examine the pictures. Look closely at the illustrations. In the first picture, which line seems longer? Is it the vertical (up and down) one? Is it the horizontal (left to right) one?

Parallel lines are the same distance apart. In the second picture, are the horizontal lines parallel? Are they the same distance apart?

The lines in the first illustration are equal. The vertical line only *looks* longer. If you don't believe it, you can measure it with a ruler. One line looks longer because it is an optical illusion. You have been deceived. Your mind has played a trick on you. The lines in the second picture are parallel. They are straight and stay the same distance apart. They do not slope toward each other or away from each other. Optical illusions prove that, sometimes, you can be tricked by what you see. It is important to think about what you see before you believe it.

1. This text is mainly about
    a. illustrations. **b.** lines. **c.** optical illusions. **d.** pictures.

2. What lines are parallel?
    a. ones that are straight and go from left to right
    b. ones that are curved and go from top to bottom
    c. ones that slope away from each other
    d. ones that are straight and stay the same distance apart

3. When you are *deceived*, you are
    a. measured. **b.** tricked. **c.** apart. **d.** examined.

4. If you see an alien spaceship in the sky,
    a. it may be an optical illusion.
    b. it has to be true.
    c. it cannot be a flat cloud.
    d. it means you need glasses.

Name: _____

Spaghetti Crop

The broadcast went on for three minutes. It was aired in Great Britain. It played over the national television station. It showed a family that was in southern Switzerland. The family was a farming family. They were harvesting spaghetti. Their trees were loaded with the dangling noodles. Some family members were on ladders. Others were holding baskets. Everyone was plucking the strands of pasta off of the tree branches.

The news segment gave two reasons for the bumper crop. First, it had been an unusually mild winter. Second, the spaghetti weevil, an insect pest that preyed on the spaghetti trees, had just about disappeared. The news reporter said, "For those who love this dish, there's nothing like real, home-grown spaghetti."

Hundreds of people called the station. They all wanted to know the same thing. They wanted to know how they could grow their own spaghetti trees. How did the station answer this query? They told everyone the same thing. They said, "Place a sprig of spaghetti into a tin of tomato sauce and hope for the best." When did this news segment air? It aired on April 1, 1957. Today, it is ranked as one of the most famous April Fool's Day pranks ever played.

1. From the text, you can tell that spaghetti
   a. is a kind of pasta.
   c. does best when growing in a mild climate.
   b. grows on trees.
   d. is best when home-grown.

2. This text is mainly about
   a. text that is broadcast.
   b. a family in southern Switzerland.
   c. an April Fool's Day trick.
   d. why the spaghetti harvest was a bumper crop.

3. A *query* is the same as a
   a. question.   b. crop.   c. insect.   d. strand.

4. What can you learn from this text?
   a. Always believe what you see on television.
   b. Nothing broadcast on April 1 is true.
   c. Switzerland is the best place to grow spaghetti.
   d. Think about what you hear and see before believing it.

5. What might have helped some people believe this story?
   a. There are few farms in Switzerland.
   c. Weevils are huge pests for farmers.
   b. The segment was aired on a cartoon channel.
   d. The broadcast was shorter than most ads.

Name: _____

More Than the News

"I left home as rapidly as I could," Aunt Sophia said. "My heart was racing, and I could feel my blood pulsing. Nothing was going to stop me!" Aunt Sophia stopped to take a sip of water. Everyone else at the table sat transfixed, anxiously waiting to find out what happened next. Aunt Sophia was a journalist, and she had traveled all over the world reporting news. Everyone loved to hear about her adventures when she came to visit.

"I got to a corner, and it looked safe, so I turned it and continued to run. I could hear screaming and shouting, but I made it to the next corner. I knew it would have been safer to stay there, but I risked it! I ran and ran until I came to another corner! I turned it and kept running, but then I saw a person with a mask!"

"What did you do then?" Sally asked, her voice horror-stricken.

"Oh," Aunt Sophia said, "I ran home. You see, I was playing baseball." There was a moment of silence before everyone began to laugh. "You see," Aunt Sophia said, "It's not just the news that counts. It's how you tell the story."

1. Why was there a moment of silence before everyone began to laugh?
   a. They were waiting for Aunt Sophia to continue with her story.
   b. They had to realize that Aunt Sophia was not in real danger.
   c. They had to stop their hearts from racing.
   d. They were waiting for the screaming and shouting to stop.

2. When people were sitting *transfixed*, they were
   a. bored and tired of the story.
   b. fascinated with and caught up in the story.
   c. thirsty and in need of a sip of water.
   d. not interested and ready to leave.

3. What did Aunt Sophia want her family to know?
   a. It is more important to make a story exciting than truthful.
   b. The facts are not important when it comes to reporting news.
   c. Journalists only care about facts.
   d. How one tells the news can change what people think about it.

4. The last corner Aunt Sophia turns is
   a. first base.   b. second base.   c. third base.   d. home plate.

5. The screaming and shouting Aunt Sophia heard most likely came from
   a. people on her team.   c. people from her home.
   b. people she was reporting on.   d. people anxious to hear the story.

Name: _____

Write On!

You watch the news on TV. Someone reports on the spaghetti harvest and on the man-eating piranhas. Share what you hear and how it is presented. Then, explain how you think you would react. Would you believe the stories? Why or why not? How would you verify, or check whether they were true? How could you convince other people that the stories were either true or fictional?

_____

_____

_____

_____

_____

_____

_____

_____

_____

_____

_____

_____

_____

_____

_____

_____

_____

_____

_____

Name: _____

Close but Unseen

A tracking device was surgically implanted in it. Then, the snake was released. The device's beeps had guided scientists through the wilds of the Florida Everglades. Now, the beeping told them that the snake was near. The scientists looked carefully, but they failed to spot it. The 16-foot snake was right in front of them! Its markings helped to camouflage it. It was only found because of the tracking device.

The snake was a python. It was not native to the Everglades. The population of the invasive species had grown to a dangerous point. Pythons were wiping out native species. They were becoming a threat to the ecosystem.

Two snake hunters from India were hired. They spent two months in the Everglades. They tracked pythons by looking for tunnels in the grass and ripples in the sand. People watched the hunters carefully. They wanted to become expert python hunters, too.

1. From the text, you can tell that pythons
   a. are a threat to India's ecosystem.
   b. can be found in India.
   c. are brightly colored.
   d. are an invasive species in India.

2. This text is mainly about
   a. looking for ripples in the sand.
   b. tracking devices.
   c. a threat to an ecosystem.
   d. how snakes camouflage themselves.

3. Where are the Everglades?
   a. India   b. France   c. Indonesia   d. Florida

4. The author first told you about the snake that had the tracking device so that you could begin to understand
   a. how hard it is to deal with the snake problem.
   b. the importance of listening.
   c. why hunters need to learn how to implant tracking devices.
   d. the population of an ecosystem.

Name: _____

Yes and No

"They are in the air about five to seven hours every day. They cover a territory of about 30,000 miles."

The students had been given "secret" jobs. They were supposed to research their jobs. Then, they were supposed to give their classmates hints. They would continue to give hints until someone guessed the job correctly.

Kaylee was sure that she already knew. "You studied pilots," she said. "You studied pilots that carry passengers to different countries. That would explain the long flight times. That would explain the number of miles."

Conner said, "Yes, I am talking about pilots. No, these pilots do not fly passenger jets. The pilots usually work from February 1 through August 31. One year, they worked from March 7 through September 26. They save lives."

No one knew what the pilots did until Conner told them. "They work for the IIP. The IIP stands for the International Ice Patrol. They track icebergs."

1. Why did Kaylee think she knew that Conner was talking about pilots who carry passengers?
   a. The pilots flew through the air.
   b. She knew pilots would also have to make the return trip.
   c. It can take hours to fly from one country to another.
   d. She had researched the same job.

2. A pilot working for the IIP would most likely NOT be flying on
   a. May 26.   b. June 14.   c. July 30.   d. December 13.

3. Most likely, what is the weather like when the IIP pilots work?
   a. cold enough for more snowfall than usual
   b. warm enough for pieces of ice to break off glaciers
   c. cold enough for the sea to freeze over
   d. the same temperature as the rest of the time

4. Most likely, what did Conner mean when he said the pilots "save lives"?
   a. They rescue people from icebergs.
   b. They drop off supplies to ships at sea.
   c. They carry icebergs to other countries.
   d. They inform ship captains as to where the icebergs are.

Name: _____

Wanted

This position opened up in 2013. Would you apply for the job?

Want to make a big splash?
This job might be perfect for you!

- Applicant needs to have strong written skills.
- Applicant must have strong verbal skills. They must speak well.
- Applicant needs to have experience in social media. They must be able to tweet. They must post videos and pictures. They must blog.
- Applicant must be willing to travel. They will need to travel through Europe. They must go to Egypt and Tunisia in Africa. They must also travel to Thailand in Asia.
- Applicant must remain flexible at all times. They must be willing to put up with unforeseen and unexpected events.
- Applicant will be paid 31,000 dollars.
- Applicant will work for six months.
- Applicant must put on a swimsuit. Then, they must twist and turn through waterslides.

A company that owned water parks posted this ad. It needed a professional waterslide tester to visit all its parks.

1. Why might someone not apply for this job?
   a. They are in a job now and will lose it if they take six months off.
   b. They like to go to water parks and enjoy slides.
   c. They think it is a lot of money to be paid to have fun.
   d. They have wanted to travel all of their lives.

2. When someone is *flexible*, he or she is
   a. ready and able to change.
   b. not afraid of water.
   c. a good writer and speaker.
   d. upset when unexpected things happen.

3. What country and continent might one have to travel to?
   a. Egypt in Europe   b. Thailand in Africa   c. Egypt in Asia   d. Tunisia in Africa

4. Most likely, why did they want the applicant to have experience with social media?
   a. so the person could keep in contact with the water park owners
   b. so the person could share the things that went wrong when testing the slides
   c. so the person could post things about his or her adventures that would make people want to go to the water parks
   d. so the person could post why one water park was better than another water park

Name: _____

The Green Wall

An entire wall panel was green. No one had painted it or purposefully made it that way. It had turned green because of the mold growing on it. At first, one may think there is an easy fix. Can't someone simply scrub the wall and replace the panel? The truth is that the green wall is only the tip of the iceberg. The problem is much greater.

The International Space Station (ISS) circles 200 miles above the Earth. It is about the size of a six-bedroom house, and it is not sterile. Astronauts bring up germs and molds. They go to the bathroom, they vomit, and they sweat. Astronauts may return to Earth, but all the microbes that they have released into the space station remain. This means that the space station hasn't had a good cleaning in over 16 years! It is like an airplane that never gets opened!

One scientist never thought that she would be an astronaut. She studied microbes. She went to remote places in Africa and studied how viruses were mutated and spread. Then, she was sent to the ISS to set up a lab. She examined microbes in the space station. She studied how they had changed and adapted.

1. What did the author mean when she said that the green wall was "only the tip of the iceberg"?
   a. The wall was once white like an iceberg but was now green.
   b. Water on the ISS was already being used for things other than cleaning.
   c. Microbes grew well on the ISS because the air was so warm.
   d. The problem was much greater than just what you could see.

2. When something is *sterile*,
   a. it has changed and adapted.
   b. it is very clean.
   c. it can be easily replaced.
   d. it is examined.

3. From the text, you can tell that the ISS has been circling Earth for about
   a. 6 days.   b. 200 days.   c. 16 years.   d. 26 years.

4. Another title for this text might be
   a. "Microbes on the ISS."
   b. "Painting Space Green."
   c. "Working in Africa and Space."
   d. "Viruses That Mutate."

5. You can tell from the text that, most likely,
   a. all of the microbes on the ISS have mutated.
   b. some of the microbes on the ISS have changed over time.
   c. none of the microbes on the ISS have adapted.
   d. most of the microbes on the ISS are dangerous.

Name: _____

Lance's First Day

On Lance's first day at his new school, he sat with some students from his class. Max told how his father had stood in line for 12 hours to get World Series tickets. Betty said that her sister waited 19 hours so that she could be first to purchase the newest cell phone. Blake said that his brother waited five hours for opening-night tickets to the movie *Big Ape*. Becca said that her mother stood in line for 14 hours to get tickets. "My mom is studying to be a lawyer," she explained. "She wants to hear a case being argued in front of the Supreme Court. The Supreme Court is the highest court in the land. It's in Washington, D.C."

When Lance said that his dad had stood in line for all those things, the other students looked at each other. Then Becca said, "You don't have to lie to make us like you." When Lance insisted he wasn't lying, the students abruptly left the table. They didn't even say "good-bye."

After lunch the teacher said, "Lance, tell us about your father's job. I hear he is a professional line sitter. Imagine being paid to stand in line!"

1. Who stood in line for five hours?
   a. the person who wanted to hear a Supreme Court case argued
   b. Blake's brother
   c. the person who purchased the newest cell phone
   d. Max's father

2. When someone acts *suddenly* and *snappishly*, he or she is
   a. professional.   b. lying.   c. abrupt.   d. insistent.

3. Most likely, why did the students feel that Lance was lying?
   a. It was Lance's first day of school.
   b. Lance was not acting professionally.
   c. The students knew that Lance wanted them to like him.
   d. Lance's father's job is not a very usual or common job.

4. What is true about the Supreme Court?
   a. It is in the state of Washington.
   b. It is the highest court in the United States.
   c. It is where people can purchase cell phones.
   d. It is where lawyers go to night school.

5. Most likely, how did the students feel at the end of the text?
   a. mad at Lance for telling the truth
   b. interested in what Lance knew about the Supreme Court
   c. sorry that they had not given Lance a chance to explain
   d. hungry because they had left the lunch table too quickly

Name: _____

Write On!

Go back through the texts in this unit. Pick any of the jobs you read about (except for the waterslide tester). Then, write a want ad for the job, using the ad for the waterslide tester as a guide.

Remember to start your ad with a catchy phrase. Think about what the job requires. You must use information from the stories, but you may also make up things like the salary, hours, and benefits.

Name: _____

Poured at Night

The Burj Khalifa, or Khalifa Tower, is in Dubai. Dubai is part of the United Arab Emirates. The tower is colossal. It soars a whopping 2,722 feet into the air.

A lot of concrete was needed to build this skyscraper. Usually, concrete is poured during the day. The concrete for this skyscraper was poured at night. In addition, ice was added to the mixture. Why was the concrete poured at night? Why was ice added to it?

The concrete had to set flawlessly. Any cracks would weaken the structure. A crack might make the concrete unable to bear the weight of all the stories above it. When a concrete mixture is cooler, it sets more evenly. It is less likely to crack. Daytime temperatures in the Persian Gulf often reach a sweltering 122°F. The concrete had to be poured at night when the outside temperature was cooler. Even then, ice still had to be added.

1. You can tell that Dubai is located in the
   a. United States of America.
   b. Persian Gulf.
   c. United Kingdom.
   d. Gulf of Aden.

2. When something is really hot, it is
   a. colossal.
   b. sweltering.
   c. flawless.
   d. whopping.

3. This text is mainly about
   a. concrete.
   b. skyscrapers.
   c. when ice is needed.
   d. concrete used in one tower.

4. What concrete would bear the most weight?
   a. the concrete on the outside of a 160-story tower
   b. the concrete in the middle of a 160-story tower
   c. the concrete at the top of a 160-story tower
   d. the concrete at the bottom of a 160-story tower

Name: _____

Walking on Water

"I know someone who walks on water," Mark said. Everyone at the lunch table burst out laughing. When Mark insisted that he was dead serious, his friends looked at each other.

Finally, Ricardo said something. "You are either talking about a hockey player or an ice skater."

Mark said, "We've been talking about records all week. We've discussed the longest, the highest, and the smallest. I looked up the record for the fastest walk across the Atlantic Ocean. It was accomplished in 1988. Remy Bricka, a man from France, performed the feat. He walked wearing skis. The skis were buoyant and floated. They were almost 14 feet long. Bricka pulled a platform of supplies and essentials. It took him 59 days. In total, he walked 3,502 miles."

"Ancient history is interesting," Chad said. He rose from the table. The other boys followed. Then, with their foot-sized air shoes, they all floated out to the playground.

1. What did Mark mean when he said that he was "dead serious"?
   a. He was not joking.
   b. People from ancient times are no longer living.
   c. He was being silly.
   d. Walking on water could be deadly.

2. Most likely, what is one of the essential items that Bricka pulled on the floating platform?
   a. a book about ancient history
   b. a pair of pajamas
   c. a water still for removing salt from seawater
   d. a vase for flowers

3. When does the author expect the reader to know that the text takes place in the future?
   a. after reading the title
   b. after reading the first paragraph
   c. after reading the second paragraph
   d. after reading the last paragraph

4. This text is fiction, but it is filled with facts. What answer is a fact?
   a. The boys wore foot-sized air shoes.
   b. Bricka walked across the Atlantic Ocean in 1988.
   c. The boys floated out to the playground.
   d. Bricka's skis were buoyant and made of iron.

Name: _____

A Play About Big and Bigger

Setting: school cafeteria
Cast (in order of appearance): 4th-grade students Lily, Rose, Daisy, Posey, Violet

Lily, Rose, and Daisy are eating lunch when Posey joins them, holding a tray.

Posey: I just saw a Great Dane, the tallest dog in the world.

Lily: That's nothing. I once saw the biggest horse in the world. His owners had to do a lot to accommodate him. Most horse stalls are 12 by 12, but his had to be 20 by 20!

Rose: That's nothing. I once saw a life-size house built with Lego blocks. It had two floors and four rooms. It was over 15 feet high, almost 20 feet wide, and 30 feet long. It took 2.4 million bricks to construct it!

Daisy: I saw something more impressive. I saw the Bhul Bhulaiya maze in India. This maze contains the most identical doorways in a maze. It has 489! It also has several staircases and 1,000 narrow passages!

*Suddenly, Violet walks over from a nearby table
and stands next to the other girls.*

Violet: I once saw four girls trying to outdo themselves with what they saw. What I now see is four girls who should come play with me before recess is over!

1. What character in the play said that she saw 489 identical doors?
   a. Violet   **b.** Lily   **c.** Rose   **d.** Daisy

2. Most likely, what is one of the props (objects used on a stage) used in this play?
   a. a school desk
   b. a menu on a wall
   c. a shelf of books
   d. a beanbag chair

3. When you *accommodate* something,
   a. you adjust or move it so it will fit.
   b. you construct or build it.
   c. you make it look the same or identical.
   d. you have to make it smaller.

4. When Violet speaks, what does she do?
   a. She only uses the past tense.
   b. She only uses the present tense.
   c. She uses the past tense and then the present tense.
   d. She uses the present tense and then the past tense.

Name: _____

On a Pin

Shaquille O'Neal is a former basketball player. He is over seven feet tall. A famous artist named Willard Wigan made a statue of O'Neal. The statue was lifelike, but it was not life size. When O'Neal went to look at it, he had to use a microscope! When O'Neal viewed himself, he said, "Put a guy like me into a little pin? That's crazy! Took him seven weeks? Probably take me 17 years!"

Although Wigan's sculptures are minute, they sell for great sums of money. Some individual pieces have sold for 150,000 dollars. Most are inside the eye of a needle or sit on a pin. No tools existed for creating such tiny pieces of art. Wigan had to improvise. What does he use for paintbrushes? He makes his own using fly hair. Another time, he plucked out his own eyelash. His eyelash became a pedestal for a statue to stand on!

Some artists may worry about falling off ladders or tripping over paint cans. They may fear cutting their hand with a chisel. In micro art, there is an entirely different class of hazards. One time, Wigan was creating a scene using characters from *Alice in Wonderland*. He accidentally inhaled a tiny Alice!

1. What is an example of something *minute*?
   a. an elephant   **b.** a school   **c.** a microbe   **d.** a house

2. This text is mainly about
   a. art.
   b. a basketball player.
   c. the dangers of art.
   d. someone who makes extremely tiny art.

3. From the text, you can tell that
   a. most of Wigan's statues stand on eyelashes.
   b. all of Wigan's pieces are inside the eye of a needle.
   c. some of Wigan's pieces take almost two months to make.
   d. none of Wigan's pieces take four months to complete.

4. Why did Wigan use fly hair for his paintbrush?
   a. Wigan couldn't buy the size paintbrush he needed.
   b. Wigan used a microscope to see the fly hair.
   c. Wigan didn't want to risk cutting himself with a chisel.
   d. Wigan didn't want to pluck out any more eyelashes.

5. Why did the author start the text by talking about Shaquille O'Neal?
   a. She wanted you to think the story was about basketball.
   b. She wanted you to contrast the size of a huge man to the miniature artwork.
   c. She wanted you to understand that many people use microscopes.
   d. She wanted you to think about how Wigan inhaled Alice.

Name: _____

A Big Difference

Anne was visiting her cousin Andre in Switzerland. Andre said, "I will take you across the Alps." Anne was excited. She loved mountains. She wondered how she would feel when they crossed over the high passes. Would she feel the effect of the altitude? Would she feel tired because there was less oxygen?

Andre and Anne got on a train. They went through a very flat, long tunnel. Andre said, "This is the Gotthard Base Tunnel. It is the longest and deepest railroad tunnel in the world. It is so deep that, without ventilation, the temperature inside the mountain would reach a sweltering 115°F. It is the first flat route through the mountain or any other major mountain range in the world."

"Wait!" Anne exclaimed. "You mean we're crossing the Alps right now? I find that hard to believe."

"It's easier to go in and through than up and over," Andre said. "What I had to experience to believe was the temperature change. The first time I went into the north portal and came out the south portal, there was a 20-degree temperature difference! Usually, the south end is only four to five degrees warmer, but some days it is a lot greater."

1. When does Anne find out that she is crossing the Alps?
   a. before she enters the tunnel
   b. as she leaves the tunnel
   c. when Andre says he will take her across the Alps
   d. while she is in the tunnel

2. From the text, you can tell that a *portal* is
   a. a kind of tunnel.   b. a flat route.   c. a type of train.   d. a doorway or entryway.

3. When would you most likely need a sweater?
   a. when you exit the tunnel on the east side
   b. when you exit the tunnel on the north side
   c. when you exit the train on the west side
   d. when you exit the tunnel on the south side

4. The title of this text refers to
   a. how breathing in high altitudes feels different.
   b. three different world tunnels.
   c. the possible temperature change between the portals.
   d. why some people find different things hard to believe.

5. What Andre said about going "in and through" only makes sense because
   a. the tunnel was already built.
   b. he was talking to one of his cousins.
   c. the tunnel was the longest and deepest in the world.
   d. it went through a major mountain range.

Name: _____

Write On!

Time to write a play! Your play must mention some of the texts or records in this unit.

If you are having trouble thinking up a plot, then write a play in which you have students discussing the stories in this unit. Have different students tell what stories they liked best and why.

Make sure your play has a title, setting, and cast. It must also have at least two stage directions.

Looking back at *A Play About Big and Bigger* will help you know how to write your title, setting, and cast. The stage directions for *A Play About Big and Bigger* are in italics. You can just put your stage directions in parentheses.

Setting: _____

Cast: _____

_____

_____

_____

_____

_____

_____

_____

_____

_____

_____

_____

_____

_____

_____

Name: _____

Where's Who?

Waldo was the brainchild of Martin Handford. Handford is an English illustrator. Handford's character wears black spectacles. He wears a red and white striped shirt. He wears a red and white striped bobbled hat, too. Handford draws elaborate and detailed scenes. Those who are observant and have a keen eye can spot Waldo somewhere in the picture.

Waldo is always dressed the same. His fame stretches across continents. It knows no country borders. Yet Waldo is not known around the world. How can that be?

Waldo is only known as Waldo in North America. In Britain, he is known as Wally. In France, Waldo is known as Charlie. In Germany, Waldo is known as Walter. In Italy, Waldo is known as Ubaldo. The Scandinavian countries also have different names for Waldo. In Norway, he is known as Willy. In Denmark, he is known as Holger. In Sweden, he is known as Hugo.

1. This text is mainly about
   a. Martin Handford.
   b. illustrations.
   c. a well-known character.
   d. what Waldo wears.

2. What country is matched to the correct name?
   a. Walter : Norway
   b. Holger : Denmark
   c. Ubaldo : France
   d. Hugo : Germany

3. When something is *elaborate*, it is
   a. complicated.   b. spectacled.   c. keen.   d. observant.

4. From the text, you can tell that
   a. identical characters have identical names.
   b. Handford's character is less known in France than in Germany.
   c. a character can have many names.
   d. In Scandinavia, Handford's character wears red and blue stripes.

Name: _____

Lifeforms

Zosa said, "There were 3,872 lifeforms. It took a while to count them because they were pretty much identical. There was a slight difference when it came to size. Other than that, they were remarkably similar. They all had black rings around their eyes. They all had red and white stripes."

"When did you take the sample?" Zosa's commander asked.

"Their calendar date said June 19, 2011. I also saw rectangular location markers. One said *Merrian Square West*. Others said *Dublin* and *Ireland*."

Zosa's commander nodded. "That's why you were sent to observe. Someone with a less keen eye would have missed the dating or location clues. Is there anything else you wish to report?"

Zosa winked its eye at the end of its tentacle. Then Zosa said, "There was a big banner. It said *Street Performance World Championship*. I also heard several of the lifeforms shouting 'Where's Wally?' I don't know why."

1. Most likely, the rectangular location markers were
    a. traffic lights.
    b. crosswalks.
    c. curbs and sidewalks.
    d. street signs.

2. Why might Zosa's report be less than accurate for lifeforms on the planet Earth?
    a. Most human beings do not dress up as Waldo or Wally.
    b. Zosa was not a keen observer.
    c. Most human beings do not wear glasses.
    d. Zosa's eye was at the end of a tentacle.

3. What can you learn about taking samples from reading this text?
    a. Only one sample is ever needed.
    b. Every sample should be taken at the same time.
    c. Every sample should be taken on the same date.
    d. It matters when and where samples are taken.

4. This text is fiction, but it includes some facts. What has to be fiction?
    a. Zosa's eye is on the end of its tentacle.
    b. 3,872 people dressed up like Waldo or Wally.
    c. The lifeforms were in Dublin, Ireland.
    d. The championship performance took place on June 19, 2011.

Name: _____

Diamante

A *diamante* is a kind of poem. In a diamante, the text forms the shape of a diamond. The instructions for each line go like this:

Line 1: Noun or subject (one word)

Line 2: Two adjectives that describe line 1

Line 3: Three gerunds (words that end in *ing*) that describe line 1

Line 4: Four nouns (the first two are connected to line 1, and the last two are connected with line 7)

Line 5: Three gerunds that describe line 7

Line 6: Two adjectives that describe line 7

Line 7: Noun synonym or similar word for the subject

Examples:

Cat	Earth
Soft, Cuddly	Round, Watery
Purring, Sleeping, Chasing	Living, Growing, Spinning
Kittens, Mice, Cubs, Deer	Humans, Farms, Deserts, Canals
Hunting, Pouncing, Biting	Stormy, Blazing, Rotating
Fierce, Powerful	Red, Dusty
Cougar	Mars

1. Most likely, this kind of poetry got its name because
   a. of the general shape the words and lines make.
   b. diamonds are hard, and these are the hardest poems in the world to write.
   c. the third person to write a poem in this form was named Diamante.
   d. you cannot eat diamonds, and you cannot eat poetry.

2. What word is not a gerund?
   a. eating   b. jumping   c. smiling   d. asleep

3. Think about how the first and last lines are related in the first poem. What other two words are related in the same way?
   a. frog and fly   c. dog and wolf
   b. chair and table   d. sheep and lamb

4. Think about how the first and last lines are related in the second poem. What other two words are related in the same way?
   a. rocket and blue   c. flower and cat
   b. Monday and Tuesday   d. January and snow

Name: _____

Wrong Side Up?

The picture had been hanging for over 47 days. Over 116,000 visitors had come to see it. Even the artist's son, who was an art dealer, had come to view it. The picture was by Henri Matisse. It was called *Le Bateau*. It was part of a special exhibition.

Genevieve Habert was not an artist. She was not a museum curator. Nor was she a member of the museum staff. She was simply a very observant spectator. After her third visit to the show, she was sure that the picture was hung upside down. To check, Habert bought a catalogue about the exhibit. She then compared the picture in the catalogue to the hanging picture. The pictures were not the same. One of them was upside down.

Habert alerted a guard. The guard was not receptive. He was not interested. He said, "You don't know what's up, and you don't know what's down, and neither do we. We can't be responsible for the printers." Habert was undeterred. She did not let the matter drop. She called a news reporter. The painting was finally flipped right side up. What did the director of exhibitions tell the reporter? He said that "it was just carelessness."

1. What is most likely true about the picture *Le Bateau*?
    a. The top is very different from the bottom.
    b. It looks very much like a mirror image.
    c. The colors on one side are much darker.
    d. It is a picture of people sitting in a boat.

2. When someone is *receptive*, he or she is
    a. alerted.   b. undeterred.   c. responsible.   d. interested.

3. This text is mainly about
    a. Henri Matisse.
    b. a picture that was incorrectly hung.
    c. what happens when people are careless.
    d. why people need to be observant.

4. Who said that it was due to carelessness that the picture was hung upside down?
    a. the guard   c. the director of exhibitions
    b. Genevieve Habert   d. the newspaper reporter

5. When did Habert buy the exhibit catalogue?
    a. the first time that she went to view the exhibit
    b. after the second time that she went to view the exhibit
    c. after the third time that she went to view the exhibit
    d. after the fourth time that she went to view the exhibit

Name: _____

The Forgery

The museum curator said, "This exhibit covers early European art. We selected the paintings with care. We wanted people to see how people lived from the 12th century to the 13th century. Most of the people were peasants then. They raised a few pigs and chickens. At that time, they did not have electricity or any of the modern conveniences we have today. They had to grow all their own food. In this picture, you can see two young children picking corn from the garden."

Tanner said, "That picture shouldn't be in this exhibit."

The museum curator said, "I'm curious as to why you think so. It just so happens that this particular painting is by a famous French painter. He was a monk, and his name was Father Claude. He mixed his own paints. He grew special plants in the monastery garden just for that purpose. Take another look at the corn in this picture. He must have used at least six different shades of green for each leaf!"

"If Father Claude's name is on that painting, then it is a forgery," Tanner said. "Corn is from the Americas. It wasn't brought to Europe until the late 15th century."

1. When something is *counterfeit* or *fake*, it is a
   a. forgery.   b. curiosity.   c. specialty.   d. variety.

2. How do you think people felt about Tanner after he called the painting a forgery?
   a. angry that he called the painting a forgery
   b. upset that he knew more than they did
   c. impressed by how observant he was
   d. tired of him talking to the curator

3. You can tell that the painting Tanner said was a forgery did not have a
   a. haystack in it.   b. tractor in it.   c. rake in it.   d. mule in it.

4. How many colors of green were in each corn leaf?
   a. less than six   b. six or less   c. exactly six   d. six or more

5. Most likely, what happens next to the painting that Tanner called a forgery?
   a. It is kept in the exhibit.
   b. It is given to Tanner.
   c. It is given back to Father Claude.
   d. It is removed from the exhibit.

Name: _____

Write On!

Write a diamante poem.

Then, rewrite your poem two more times. The first time, flip the top and bottom lines only.

The second time, rewrite it so that all the words are written in the reverse order. Your last word becomes your first word. Your second-to-last word becomes your second word—and so on.

Read one version to the class. Did anyone notice that the poem was written incorrectly? Did the order of the words matter?

_____

_____ , _____

_____ , _____ , _____

_____ , _____ , _____ , _____

_____ , _____ , _____

_____ , _____

_____

_____

_____ , _____

_____ , _____ , _____

_____ , _____ , _____ , _____

_____ , _____ , _____

_____ , _____

_____

_____

_____ , _____

_____ , _____ , _____

_____ , _____ , _____ , _____

_____ , _____ , _____

_____ , _____

_____

Name: _____

Sailing Stones

There are rocks from Europe in Africa. The stones came from Portugal, a southern European country on the Atlantic Ocean. The stones were brought to Mozambique. Mozambique is a southeastern African country on the Indian Ocean. The stones were carried on sailing ships back in the 1500s. Why were stones carried from one continent to another?

The Portuguese first landed in Mozambique in 1492. When they landed, they saw that they could grow rich from trade. Before they left Portugal, they filled the bottom of their ships with stones. This was for ballast. The stones made the ship heavier and helped balance it. When the Portuguese got to Mozambique, they didn't need the stones. They filled the ship with trade goods instead.

The stones were not thrown away. They were used in the forts the Portuguese built along the coast. Tourists can still see some of these forts today. They can touch stones that are far from home.

1. Mozambique is
   a. on the Pacific Ocean.
   b. on the Indian Ocean.
   c. on the Atlantic Ocean.
   d. on the Arctic Ocean.

2. This text is mainly about
   a. rocks.
   b. two continents.
   c. trading in the 1500s.
   d. stones used by the Portuguese.

3. If a ship started to sink, the captain could
   a. order the stones to be thrown overboard.
   b. carry the stones to the front part of the ship.
   c. carry the stones to the back part of the ship.
   d. place the stones evenly around the deck.

4. Stones from Mozambique are less likely to be found in Portugal
   a. because no forts were built in Portugal.
   b. because cargo planes now transport trade goods.
   c. because stones were not needed for ballast.
   d. because Mozambique is a sandy country.

Name: _____

World's Smallest

Angel was playing a game with his classmates. As soon as he said that his country is home to the world's smallest mammal, Mike raised his hand. "I know what country you are thinking of already," he said. "It has to be Brazil. The Amazon rainforest is there. Brazil is rich in flora and fauna. New plants and animals are still being discovered there."

Terri interrupted. She said, "Your country has to be Cuba. You're talking about the bee hummingbird. That bird is the world's smallest avian creature. It's only about the size of a bumblebee!"

Angel said, "You're forgetting that although birds are animals, they are not mammals. I was talking about Kitti's hog-nosed bat. It wasn't discovered until the 1970s. It's barely an inch long, and it weighs less than a penny. The bee hummingbird can hover. The wings of the hog-nosed bat seem to be adapted for hovering flight, too. My country is Thailand. Thailand is in Southeast Asia."

1. Most likely, what game was Angel's class playing?
   a. Name That Mammal!
   b. Name That Continent!
   c. Name That Country!
   d. Name That Animal!

2. What would not be part of Thailand's flora?
   a. the Mulberry tree
   b. water buffalo
   c. bamboo
   d. coconut palms

3. A country's *fauna* refers to
   a. that country's mammals.
   b. that country's mammals and flora.
   c. that country's avian creatures.
   d. all animals in that country.

4. Where is Thailand?
   a. South America
   b. Asia
   c. Southeast Africa
   d. Australia

Name: _____

Hugs from Chile

Hotel de Santiago

January 15

Dear Carrie,

   The week has flown by! We've had nothing but adventures in the longest and narrowest country in the world. We've seen glaciers, deserts, mountains, and volcanoes. No matter where I go, I'm never afraid. That's because there aren't any bears or poisonous snakes here.

   Did I tell you about the weather? In my home city of Boston, there is two feet of snow. Here, it is not winter. It's balmy and warm! That's because it's summer here. Boston is in the Northern Hemisphere. Here in the Southern Hemisphere, seasons are the opposite. In Boston, spring begins in March. Here, it begins in September. Summer begins in December, and winter begins in June.

   Tomorrow, we're going to see the world's largest picture of a person. The picture is hundreds of years old. It's nearly 400 feet long. It's a geoglyph. It was made by scraping away the top layer of stones to reveal lighter sand underneath.

   A huge hug all the way from Chile,

   Nina

1. In Chile, July would be a
   a. winter month.   **b.** spring month.   **c.** summer month.   **d.** fall month.

2. When the weather is *balmy*, it is
   a. freezing and icy.   **b.** snowy and cold.   **c.** pleasant and mild.   **d.** rainy and windy.

3. You can tell that the world's largest picture of a man
   a. is in the jungle.   **b.** is on the ground.   **c.** is in a museum.   **d.** is in a cave.

4. Most likely, what is the relationship between Carrie and Nina?
   a. They are friends.
   b. They are mother and daughter.
   c. They barely know each other.
   d. They are grandmother and granddaughter.

Name: _____

Two Caves

There is a country with two caves. Four boys discovered the first cave in 1940 when their dog fell down a hole. The boys climbed in after their dog and found hundreds of prehistoric animals painted on the walls and the ceiling. The paintings were over 17,000 years old, but they were in pristine condition. The colors were vibrant and fresh.

About 40 years later, another cave was opened. This cave was built right next to the first cave. It was an exact replica. It was the same size. It had the same paintings and etchings on the walls. It cost 64 million dollars, but everyone was glad that the new cave was built. Today, very few people enter the first cave. They happily enter the second cave. Where are these two caves, and why is one a replica of the other?

The caves are in France. They are known as the Lascaux Caves. The original cave was being destroyed because there were too many visitors. Their exhaled carbon dioxide and body heat were ruining the paintings! The cave was sealed up like it was before in order to preserve the artwork. Only researchers can enter it now. Everyone else enjoys the artwork in the duplicate cave.

1. Most likely, the original paintings looked fresh and new because
   a. they had been recently painted.
   b. it was steamy and hot inside the cave.
   c. the four boys didn't touch the walls when they explored the cave.
   d. the cave was sealed and dry until the dog fell through.

2. When the people were exhaling carbon dioxide, they were
   a. looking at the paintings.
   b. breathing out.
   c. looking at the etchings.
   d. sweating.

3. The replica cave opened in what year?
   a. 1947   b. 1965   c. 1983   d. 2004

4. A *replica* is the same as
   a. a discovery.   b. a duplicate.   c. an etching.   d. something vibrant.

5. From the text, you can tell that
   a. a lot of people wanted to view the prehistoric artwork.
   b. researchers were only interested in the age of the paintings.
   c. very few people have entered the original cave.
   d. the Lascaux Cave is one of the biggest caves in France.

Name: _____

The Island

Mrs. Miller said, "I'm buying the plane tickets today. You have to tell me where you want to go for vacation." Mr. Miller started to speak, but just then, all the children started clamoring for attention. The noise they made was a terrible din. It was so loud that Mrs. Miller couldn't hear what Mr. Miller was saying. Over and over again, she kept asking him to repeat himself. Mr. Miller was already late for work, so he quickly scribbled down where he wanted to go and then raced out the door.

When the Miller family was in the air, Mr. Miller said, "I have been looking forward to seeing volcanoes all my life. Best of all, since it's June, it will never get dark. There will only be a brief time of twilight." Mrs. Miller looked at Mr. Miller strangely.

When the plane landed, the Miller family stepped off onto an island. There were no volcanoes. The sun set at night. Mr. Miller had wanted to go to an island, but he was on the wrong one! He had had wanted to go to Iceland. Mrs. Miller said, "Your penmanship needs work. I thought that you wrote *Ireland*."

1. Most likely, how did Mr. Miller feel at the end of the text?
   a. pleasantly surprised
   b. happy that he was on an island
   c. angry and ready to go back home
   d. upset but able to laugh

2. What action would create a din?
   a. pounding on a soft pillow
   b. whispering to a friend next to you
   c. someone singing a goodnight song to a baby
   d. banging two metal trashcan lids together over and over

3. This text is mainly about
   a. a surprise due to a misunderstanding.
   b. penmanship.
   c. the difference between two islands.
   d. why children should be quiet.

4. What do you know for sure about the Millers?
   a. They were taking their vacation in June.
   b. They had five children.
   c. Both Mr. and Mrs. Miller worked.
   d. They had never been on an airplane before.

5. When does the reader get a hint that the Miller family might not be going where Mr. Miller wants?
   a. when Mr. Miller says that he has always wanted to see volcanoes
   b. when Mrs. Miller said that she was buying the plane tickets
   c. when Mrs. Miller looks at Mr. Miller strangely
   d. when the children started to clamor for attention

Name: _____

Write On!

Write a letter to someone by using the letter in this unit as a model. Put in a location, date, greeting, and farewell. Choose one country from each text that is in this unit. Then, tell the person to whom you are writing one thing you learned about each country.

For your final paragraph, tell what country you would most like to visit and why.

_____

_____

_____

_____

_____

_____

_____

_____

_____

_____

_____

_____

_____

_____

_____

_____

_____

_____

_____

_____

_____

_____

Name: _____

Riddle Sound

The sounds can be very frightening. In some places, they sound like moans. In other places, they bellow. Yet in other places, the sound has been described as a rumble of distant thunder. In ancient times, people thought that it was evil spirits. It was a riddle that took science to explain.

The sounds come from sand. Not all sand dunes produce these frightening sounds. Conditions have to be right. It also depends on the individual size of the grains as well as what is underneath.

Scientists stuck probes deep into one of the singing dunes. They found concrete-hard layers deep beneath the surface. Stepping on a dune crest or even the blowing of a strong wind could trigger an avalanche. The noise of the tumbling grains is amplified because of the hard layers underneath. The result is a droning noise that can last for up to a minute after the sand has stopped moving!

1. Why didn't the author immediately tell you where the sounds were coming from?
    a. She wanted to first talk about what is under the surface.
    b. She wanted to scare you and make you afraid.
    c. She wanted you to think about how sounds are amplified.
    d. She wanted to make you curious so that you would be interested.

2. What could cause a dune to start bellowing?
    a. a strong wind
    b. stepping on the bottom
    c. an evil spirit
    d. normal conditions

3. What is true about sand dunes that "sing"?
    a. Every sand dune can produce sound.
    b. One may hear the sound when the sand is completely still.
    c. They all sound the same.
    d. One can only hear the sound when the sand is moving.

4. In ancient times, why might people crossing singing sands be terrified?
    a. They did not know that there was a scientific explanation.
    b. They did not have probes to stick into the sand.
    c. They did not want to hurt themselves on the hard layer.
    d. They did not know why they only heard the sounds at night.

Name: _____

Making It Fun

Isabella cried out in frustration, "I can't take it! The task is too arduous and terribly difficult. I don't want to memorize the names of all these countries. I just want to have fun!"

Hiroto said, "You're making a mountain out of a molehill. I know you're good at riddles, so I'll ask you some riddles in order to make you feel better." Hiroto spoke slowly and clearly as he asked, "What country is made of metal? What country wants more food? What country is not hot? What country goes well with toast? What country is oily?"

Frowning, Isabella scanned the list of countries she had to memorize. Then, a light went off in her head, and a broad smile spread across her face. "Canada, Hungary, Chile, Jamaica, and Greece!" she cried triumphantly. "Now, you tell me what country hurts and what country is really loud?"

"S**pain** and **BANG**ladesh!" Hiroto said, emphasizing the clue parts of the word.

1. This text is mainly about
    a. why Isabella liked to memorize.
    b. how to spell countries' names.
    c. different countries with mountains.
    d. turning a task into something fun.

2. What did Hiroto mean when he told Isabella she was "making a mountain out of a molehill"?
    a. She was making a mountain.
    b. She was making too much out of a small thing.
    c. She was playing instead of working.
    d. She was right to be frustrated.

3. When something is really difficult, it is
    a. broad.   b. arduous.   c. scanned.   d. emphasized.

4. One riddle asks, "*What country goes well with toast?*" Why does the given answer work?
    a. You eat toast when you are hungry.
    b. Butter comes in cans.
    c. You put JAM on your toast.
    d. People like greasy food.

Name: _____

School Bus

Look at this picture of the school bus. Now, decide what direction the bus is going. Is it going to the left or to the right? Is it even possible to tell?

Most children under the age of ten answered correctly immediately. Adults had a much more difficult time deciding. If they could decide, it took them a lot longer. Researchers feel this is because children relied on the very first visual clue that their brain keyed in on. Adults, on the other hand, are used to taking in many visual and sensory clues and then basing their decisions on experience.

The answer depends on where one lives. If one lives in the United Kingdom, the bus is traveling to the right. If one lives in the United States, the bus is traveling to the left. The key visual clue is that the bus does not have any doors. This means that one must infer that the door is on the other side, closest to the sidewalk. In the United Kingdom, cars drive on the left-hand side of the road. In the United States, cars drive on the right-hand side of the road.

1. What is the key visual clue when solving this puzzle?
   a. The bus does not have a driver.
   b. The bus is empty.
   c. The bus does not have doors.
   d. The bus has windows.

2. Why does where you live affect how you answer?
   a. Cars don't drive on the same side of the road in every country.
   b. Cars drive on the right side of the road in every country.
   c. Sidewalks are only on the left side of the road.
   d. Some buses have front and rear doors.

3. When looking at the picture, what is one thing an adult is likely NOT looking for?
   a. road signs
   b. distance between the windows
   c. rear turning lights
   d. yellow shoes

4. When people *conclude or decide something based on the information they took in*, they
   a. are visualizing it.   b. are inferring it.   c. are sensing it.   d. are proving it.

Name: _____

Why the Chicken?

Why did the chicken cross the road? Unless you have been hiding under a rock for the last 100 years, you know the answer. The correct response is "to get to the other side." No one knows exactly how old this joke is, but it was printed in a New York City monthly magazine in 1847. The magazine was called *The Knickerbocker.*

There are many variations of this riddle. One might be asked why the turkey crossed the road twice. The answer is "to prove that he's no chicken." Or one might be asked why the elephant crossed the road. The answer is "because it was the chicken's day off." Curious as to why the dinosaur crossed the road? The answer is "because chickens didn't exist yet."

Some variations of these jokes are puns. Puns are jokes that play on word sounds or meanings. Two examples of puns are "Why did the chicken cross the playground?" and "Why did the whale cross the ocean?" The answer to the former is "to get to the other slide." The answer to the latter is "to get to the other tide."

1. A *response* is

    a. a pun.   **b.** an answer.   **c.** a joke.   **d.** a riddle.

2. If people talked about two things, the
    a. first thing they talked about would be the latter.
    b. second thing they talked about would be the former.
    c. second thing they talked about would be the latter.
    d. last thing they talked about would be the former.

3. *The Knickerbocker* came out

    a. daily.   **b.** weekly.   **c.** monthly.   **d.** yearly.

4. What did the author mean when she wrote "hiding under a rock for the last 100 years"?
    a. The reader was hiding under a rock.
    b. Someone hadn't been paying attention to anything around them.
    c. It is hard to think about jokes when weighed down.
    d. You are someone who does not like riddles or jokes.

5. Why is the riddle about the chicken crossing the playground a *pun*?
    a. It is a variation of an old riddle.
    b. Chickens do not play.
    c. The answer is very funny.
    d. The word *slide* almost sounds like *side*.

Name: _____

50 Percent Chance

A greedy king thought of a way to amass more gold. "I will write 'YES' on one card and 'NO' on another," he said. "The cards will go in a bag, and for a fee of 50 gold coins, anyone can draw one card out. If a young man draws the 'YES' card, he wins my daughter's hand. The cards will be drawn in front of the entire court so that there can be no cheating. Losing is proof that that you didn't deserve my daughter."

Kings and princes came from far and wide. They all drew the "NO" card. "You must not be good enough," the king would say with a sad face—as he pocketed his gold. The truth was that the dishonest king had printed "NO" on both cards!

Then, one day a hard-working and intelligent peasant named Santiago arrived. Santiago said that although he didn't have the fee, he would become the king's slave if he lost. Thinking of all the free labor he would receive, the king quickly said yes. How is it possible the story ends with Santiago marrying the princess?

Santiago tore up his card immediately after drawing it and threw the pieces into the wind. The king was forced to read the card that remained in the bag.

1. Why did Santiago tear up his card?
   a. The king could not admit to cheating so if the king's card said NO, Santiago's had to say YES.
   b. Santiago hoped that, if the card was torn up, the king would forget about him becoming a slave.
   c. He didn't want people to think that the king was dishonest.
   d. Santiago was so nervous about losing that he tore up the card without thinking.

2. When you *amass* something, you
   a. deserve it.   b. get a lot of it.   c. give it away.   d. get it immediately.

3. A *50 percent chance* of being able to marry the princess is the same as a
   a. one in two chance.   c. one in four chance.
   b. one in three chance.   d. one in five chance.

4. From the outcome of the text, you can tell that
   a. Santiago was not as smart as the king.   c. Santiago did not mind if he was a slave.
   b. Santiago had figured out how the king was cheating.   d. Santiago came from far away.

5. Why did the king make the face he did when he pocketed the fees the kings and princes paid?
   a. He wanted free labor instead of the gold.
   b. He was unhappy no one was going to marry his daughter.
   c. He was pretending.
   d. He was upset that the kings had come from far and wide.

Write On!

First, explain what a riddle is. Tell whether there can be both fiction and nonfiction riddles. Defend your answer with information from the stories in this unit.

Next, explain whether it's possible for a riddle to help one to learn facts and to think critically. Once again, defend your answer by using information from the stories in this unit.

Finally, explain the following pun to someone who is learning how to speak English: *Why are teddy bears never hungry?* They are always stuffed!

_____

_____

_____

_____

_____

_____

_____

_____

_____

_____

_____

_____

_____

_____

_____

_____

_____

_____

_____

_____

_____

Name: _____

Unfit to Drink

How is it possible that a person can be surrounded by water and yet suffer from thirst? Divide the Earth's surface into 100 parts. About 71 of those parts are water. Despite 71 percent of the Earth's surface being water, the vast majority of it is salt water. Only a small percentage is fresh water. Humans can only drink fresh water.

Why can't humans drink salt water? After all, it's cool and wet, and it can make a parched mouth feel moist. The truth is that the relief will only be temporary. Ocean water is nearly four times saltier than the fluids in your body. People have two kidneys. These organs work to flush out extra salt from our bodies. Kidneys need fresh water to flush out the salt. When you drink salt water, your kidneys need more fresh water to flush out the excess salt. The more salt water you drink, the thirstier you get.

1. When something is *parched*, it is
   - **a.** moist.
   - **b.** surrounded.
   - **c.** temporary.
   - **d.** dry.

2. From the text, you can tell that
   - **a.** our kidneys are more important than other organs.
   - **b.** our body fluids are 71 percent salt.
   - **c.** our kidneys need eight glasses of fresh water a day.
   - **d.** our bodies need to maintain a certain salt level.

3. The main idea of this text is that
   - **a.** our kidneys flush out excess salt.
   - **b.** Earth's surface is mostly water.
   - **c.** drinking salt water makes one thirstier.
   - **d.** ocean water is salty.

4. If you feel thirsty after eating pizza, it may be because
   - **a.** the pizza was ordered from the store.
   - **b.** the pizza was not well cooked.
   - **c.** the pizza was made with lots of salt.
   - **d.** the pizza did not have any mushrooms.

Name: _____

The Important Guest

Mason looked at the medieval tapestry that was on the wall. It showed a lord and his guests feasting in a castle. Mason said, "I can tell who the most important guest is."

Mason's friend Brett scoffed. "Seeing as how this is the 21st century, and you were not alive during the 5th through 15th centuries, I seriously doubt you can."

Mason pointed and said, "That man is. He's by the lord and the guest closest to the salt. Salt at that time was a valuable commodity. Long ago, people didn't have refrigeration or ways to keep food fresh. Salt was a great food preservative, and it had the added quality of making food taste better. If a man was seated where he could easily reach it, it was a sign of his importance."

Brett said, "The value of a commodity sure can change. Today, salt is cheap. In fact, it's the least expensive spice in the store!"

1. What century is part of the Medieval Ages?
   a. the 14th century
   b. the 17th century
   c. the 19th century
   d. the 21st century

2. A good or thing that can be traded is a
   a. tapestry.   b. preservative.   c. commodity.   d. sign.

3. What statement does not explain why salt is cheaper today?
   a. We have other ways to preserve food.
   b. We use it to make food taste better.
   c. We can transport it easily around the world.
   d. We have found easier ways of getting it in a useable form.

4. Most likely, Mason and Brett were
   a. in school.
   b. in a grocery store.
   c. at a zoo.
   d. in an art museum.

Name: _____

Rubbing Salt

Rubbing salt in the wound is an idiom. An idiom is a group of words that have a meaning that you couldn't deduce from the meanings of the individual words. Using only what the individual words mean, *rubbing salt in the wound* means that salt was rubbed in a wound. Ouch! That would hurt! But the phrase means something completely different. It means to make a difficult or bad situation even worse.

Perhaps you woke up early and couldn't get back to sleep. Finding out it is a holiday only rubs salt in the wound. Perhaps you were late to lunch. You were already upset about having less time to play. Then, the person in front of you gets the last dessert! You missing out on dessert is like rubbing salt in an open wound!

What is the origin of this phrase? Centuries ago, sailors were forced into service. Punishment at sea was harsh. At times sailors were lashed on the back. Often, the whip would break open their skin. Salt was rubbed into their wounds. This hurt terribly. Long ago, people did not have the medicines we have today. Salt was a valuable antiseptic. It was used to help prevent infection.

1. The *origin* of something is
   a. what it means.
   b. when it is used.
   c. why it is important.
   d. how it began.

2. *It is raining cats and dogs*
   a. means that it is raining cats and dogs.
   b. is an idiom meaning that it is raining heavily.
   c. means that cats and dogs are chasing each other.
   d. is an idiom meaning that cats and dogs will never get along.

3. Why might a doctor tell someone to gargle with salt water?
   a. Salt is a natural antiseptic.
   b. Salt tastes good.
   c. Salt is as valuable as expensive medicine.
   d. Salt will make your mouth sting.

4. Most likely, the idiom "worth his salt" or "worth her salt" means
   a. that he or she likes to add salt to their food.
   b. that he or she is valuable.
   c. that he or she weighs more than salt.
   d. that he or she does not know what salt is.

Name: _____

All About Tears

Our eyes produce three types of tears. *Basal tears* are in our eyes all the time. They lubricate, nourish, and protect our corneas. The cornea is the eye's clear, protective outer layer. Basal tears act as a shield. They help to keep dirt and other debris away from our eyes.

If someone is chopping onions or is around smoke, he or she will produce *reflex tears*. Reflex tears wash away harmful irritants. They are produced in larger amounts than basal tears. Reflex tears may contain more antibodies to help fight bacteria. *Emotional tears* are different. These tears are a response to joy or sadness. They flow when we feel sadness and other emotional states. Emotional tears contain more hormones than basal or reflex tears. Hormones are made in our bodies. They affect how we act, feel, or grow.

All of our tears are salty. When we cry, our tears do not irritate or make our eyes hurt. Why is it then that, when we open our eyes while swimming underwater in the ocean, our eyes sting? Shouldn't our eyes be used to the salt? The reason lies in the concentration. Seawater contains about three times more salt than our tears. The higher concentration of salt causes our eyes to sting.

1. If a bug lands in your eye, your eye will produce
   a. basal tears.   **b.** reflex tears.   **c.** emotional tears.   **d.** hormonal tears.

2. How do some tears act as a shield?
   a. They help to keep dirt and other debris from the eyes.
   b. They have a high concentration of salt.
   c. They are a response to joy and sadness.
   d. They protect the cornea from hormones.

3. An *irritant* is something that
   a. protects you.   **b.** aids you.   **c.** bothers you.   **d.** nourishes you.

4. The Dead Sea is almost ten times saltier than the ocean. From this, you can infer that the water in the Dead Sea
   a. would not sting your eyes.
   b. would sting your eyes less than the ocean's.
   c. would sting your eyes the same as the ocean's.
   d. would sting your eyes more than the ocean's.

5. From the text, you can tell that if we see an animal shedding tears
   a. it means that the animal is sad.
   b. it must be a sign that the animal is in an emotional state.
   c. it means that the animal is afraid.
   d. it may not mean that the animal is sad.

Name: _____

The Magic Lamp

When Sasha was walking home from school, she saw something glinting by a tree root. Attracted by its shine, she bent down and extracted it by scraping off the dirt. It appeared to be an odd-shaped lamp. "Maybe it is magic," Sasha thought with amusement, as she rubbed it clean with the edge of her shirt.

Suddenly, a genie appeared! "I've been in that thing for centuries!" the genie said. "My, how the world has changed! What kind of animal is that?" he asked, pointing to a car. "That doesn't look like a camel, and why isn't the ground sandy?"

"I wish for my backpack to be filled with treasure!" Sasha said quickly. "Do that one thing, and you are free forever." The genie nodded, and suddenly Sasha's backpack became so heavy that she nearly bent under its weight. Thinking of her wealth and all her riches, she raced home as quickly as she could. Her excitement turned to woe when she opened her backpack.

It was filled with slabs of salt. "Salt!" Sasha cried out in anguish. "What's so precious about salt?" Then, she remembered her history. In ancient times, huge camel caravans traveled across the African deserts in order to trade gold for salt.

1. What title best sums up this text?
   a. "A Camel and a Backpack."
   b. "A Genie and a Car."
   c. "Ancient Treasure and a Wish."
   d. "Centuries and a Caravan."

2. When a person feels *woe,* he or she feels
   a. rich or wealthy.
   b. excited or thrilled.
   c. anguish or sorrow.
   d. amused or entertained.

3. How do you know Sasha really didn't expect the lamp to be a magic lamp?
   a. It was under a tree root and needed to be extracted.
   b. She was hopeful when she thought about it being magic.
   c. It was odd-shaped and dirty.
   d. She was amused when she thought about it being magic.

4. Most likely, the genie
   a. thought that he was giving Sasha real treasure.
   b. didn't want to make Sasha's wish come true.
   c. was angry that Sasha had found the lamp.
   d. had only been in the lamp for one century.

5. This text is fiction, but it has one fact in it. What statement is a fact?
   a. Gold was once traded for salt.
   b. Genies once lived in lamps.
   c. Sasha let the genie go free.
   d. Sasha's backpack was filled with slabs of salt.

Name: _____

Write On!

You are stranded on a deserted island. Would you rather be left with a backpack full of gold or a backpack full of salt? Give reasons why you think one would be better. When you give reasons about salt, you must use information from the texts. Finally, explain which one you would pick and why.

_____

_____

_____

_____

_____

_____

_____

_____

_____

_____

_____

_____

_____

_____

_____

_____

_____

_____

_____

_____

_____

Name: _____

Shipwrecked

They docked near McMurdo Sound in January 1915. Their goal was to set food caches 60 miles apart. If they didn't, their leader and his men would die. The expedition's leader was Sir Ernest Shackleton. Shackleton was on the other side of Antarctica. His goal was to cross the continent. No one had ever done it before. Shackleton could not carry enough supplies on his sleds. If he was to survive, the men near McMurdo Sound had to deposit food and fuel. They had to make the caches!

Disaster struck! The men's ship was blown away in a fierce storm. They had little food. Three men died, but the men made the caches. The surviving seven, cold and hungry, huddled in a flimsy hut for a year. When rescued, they were told that their endeavor had been done in vain. Shackleton never even made it onto the continent! His ship had been crushed by the ice!

1. How many men, in total, worked to set up the caches starting near McMurdo Sound?
   a. five　　　　　　**b.** seven　　　　　　**c.** ten　　　　　　**d.** thirteen

2. From the story, you can tell that Shackleton
   a. had crossed the continent before.
   b. had planned his route before setting out.
   c. knew when disaster had struck his men at McMurdo Sound.
   d. did not trust the men at McMurdo Sound to make the caches.

3. When someone *caches* something, he or she
   a. uses it immediately.
   b. hides it on a docked ship.
   c. puts it on a sled.
   d. stores it for future use.

4. What type of men were the ones at McMurdo Sound?
   a. responsible and willing to put themselves second
   b. selfish and only thinking of themselves
   c. greedy and only caring about their next meal
   d. cautious and not willing to take risks

Name: _____

Stranded!

"I must not show fear. I must not show fear. I must not show fear," Donald chanted repeatedly to himself. The words didn't help when Donald heard the ferocious roar of a tiger. "Avoid the tiger at all costs," Donald said, picking up his speed.

Donald continued to charge ahead until he was forced to stop short. A huge elephant was blocking his path! "I really don't like being lost," Donald muttered to himself. "What if I die of thirst before I'm found? First things first—when stranded, find a source of clean water because water is essential to survival!"

"There!" Donald said triumphantly. "A source of water!" He hustled over, bent down, and drank greedily. While quenching his thirst, he felt something hit his shoulder.

Donald was fearful of what he might find, but he relaxed once he turned. "Have you seen the snow leopard exhibit yet?" his friend Mitchell asked excitedly. "This zoo is amazing!"

1. Most likely, what did Donald feel hit his shoulder?
   a. the elephant's trunk
   b. his friend tapping him
   c. a leaf from a jungle plant
   d. some water droplets

2. When someone *stops short,* he or she
   a. stops suddenly.
   b. stops and bends down.
   c. stops and goes a step backward.
   d. stops and turns.

3. When you *quench* something, you
   a. lost it.   b. satisfy it.   c. fear it.   d. strand it.

4. Why wasn't this text called "Stranded at the Zoo"?
   a. It would make you worry that Donald couldn't survive.
   b. It doesn't tell you who or what was stranded.
   c. It does not give enough essential information.
   d. It would take away the surprise ending.

Name: _____

Castaway's Diary

Day 4

Why someone would put pens and a notebook of paper in a survival kit, I don't know. I will keep track of the days I am here by writing a daily journal. My boat sank during a storm, and I do not know exactly how long I was in the life raft, as I was unconscious part of the time.

Day 14

My raft is now the roof of my shelter. I built up the sides with driftwood I pulled up from the beach. I feel fortunate to have found this spring, but somehow, I have to figure out how to catch some fish. I can only eat so many coconuts!

Day 725

I ran out of food this morning, but fortunately, I have become quite a skilled fisherman. I never thought I would be on this island for so long. However, I no longer live a life of solitude. I found Francesca abandoned in her nest with a broken wing. When I first spoke to her, I was startled by the sound of my own voice.

1. By the time of the final diary entry above, approximately how many years has the castaway been stranded on the island?
   - **a.** 2
   - **b.** 14
   - **c.** 4
   - **d.** 7

2. The reader can infer that the castaway is on an island where it is warm because
   - **a.** his raft floated up there.
   - **b.** birds live on it.
   - **c.** of the kind of trees on the island.
   - **d.** there is running water on it.

3. When someone is *marooned*, he or she is
   - **a.** surviving.
   - **b.** startled.
   - **c.** stranded.
   - **d.** solitary.

4. Most likely, the castaway
   - **a.** is only eating coconuts.
   - **b.** figured out how to catch fish.
   - **c.** drank all the water in the spring.
   - **d.** lives on an island where no other animals live.

Name: _____

18 Years

Captain Nidever landed on San Nicolas in 1853. San Nicolas is a small island off the coast of California. The ship's crew discovered footprints on the beach. They also found a piece of seal blubber that had been left out to dry. The signs of habitation led to a search. A lone Native American woman was found. She had survived in complete solitude for 18 years.

The woman showed the sailors her hut. It was crude and rough. She had used whale bones to construct it. She showed them a cave that she sheltered in at times, too. The crew saw her hooks made out of seashells. They saw the grass baskets she had woven. They saw the clothes she had made out of seabird feathers and seal skins.

The woman eagerly sailed with the captain to Santa Barbara. She stayed in a mission there. She told her story by using sign language, as no one understood her language. Most of her tribe had been slaughtered by hostile hunters in 1814. In 1835, the remaining members of her tribe were picked up. Somehow, she was left stranded. Her story of surviving in complete isolation was fictionalized in the book *Island of the Blue Dolphins*.

1. The text does not tell
   a. what the woman used for fishhooks.
   c. where the woman was taken.
   b. when the woman was found.
   d. why the woman was left stranded.

2. When you are *isolated*, you are
   a. on an island.   b. signing.   c. discovered.   d. apart from others.

3. This text is mainly about
   a. a woman who lived in solitude.
   c. islands off California.
   b. Native Americans.
   d. the book *Island of the Blue Dolphins*.

4. How do you know that the woman left willingly with the captain?
   a. She showed him her hut.
   c. She was eager to go.
   b. She swam to his boat.
   d. She gave him some fishhooks.

5. What can you tell about the woman from the text?
   a. She was hungry most of the time.
   b. She enjoyed living in solitude.
   c. She was strong in mind and body.
   d. She was twenty years old when she was saved.

Name: _____

Rescued!

"Captain, you're not going to believe this. Our instruments are showing a lifeform. It has a carbon base." The captain's eyebrow arched as she leaned over the navigator's shoulder to check for herself.

"Analysis shows it to be human," she said. "Unbelievable! This base was abandoned years ago. Do you think a person was forgotten? We had better check it out. Prepare to descend," she ordered the navigator.

The ship made its descent. It landed gently on the dusty, red soil. "The lifeform is moving away from the ship!" the navigator said. "Perhaps it thinks we are hostile.

"Perhaps it has lost its mind. This base was abandoned over 20 years ago. Complete solitude can affect people in strange ways. Some people go crazy. Others have hallucinations. They see things that aren't there. They hear imaginary voices. I'll send a team of four. Move with extreme caution."

The team put on suits. They exited the spacecraft carefully. They tracked the lifeform by using their instruments and moved toward it. They found it huddled behind a rock. The team member who reached it first spoke in a gentle voice. "We've come to rescue you."

"Leave me alone!" the human being cried. "I came all the way to Mars to be alone!"

1. This text would be considered
    a. factual.   **b.** a folktale.   **c.** science fiction.   **d.** autobiographical.

2. From the text, you cannot tell for certain if the captain
    a. had a crew of at least four.   **c.** knew if Mars had ever been visited before.
    b. is cautious.   **d.** is human.

3. Someone might say you are *hallucinating* if
    a. you think there is a monster under your bed.
    b. you think you hear a monster under your bed.
    c. you are afraid of a monster under your bed.
    d. you see a monster under your bed.

4. When something *descends*, it
    a. arches.   **b.** goes down.   **c.** huddles.   **d.** exits.

5. This text is mainly about
    a. finding someone at an abandoned base.
    b. space travel.
    c. why some people do not want to be rescued.
    d. what happens to people in solitude.

Name: _____

Write On!

Imagine that you are one of the characters from one of the stories in this unit. Write two diary entries. Use the word "I," as you will be writing as that character. The information that you include in your diary entry must match the facts from the story. For example, if you are writing as the woman from San Nicolas, you cannot mention space ships! You might write about how you found the whale bones for your shelter.

Date: _____

_____

_____

_____

_____

_____

_____

_____

_____

_____

_____

Date: _____

_____

_____

_____

_____

_____

_____

_____

_____

_____

_____

Name: _____

The Wrestler

It was Anthony Robles's first wrestling match. He was a high school freshman, and he was the smallest member on the team. It was the custom for the team to run out at the beginning of a competition and circle the mat. When Anthony did, it wasn't his small size that people noticed. It was that everyone else ran. Anthony hopped.

Anthony was born with only one leg. When Anthony started to wrestle, he wasn't very good. He lost his first match and most of the rest. Yet he became known as "unstoppable." In practice, he would always challenge the best wrestler on his team. He always strove to improve. His attitude made the coaches pay attention to him. Together, they worked on moves that were advantageous to a wrestler missing a limb.

Anthony went on to wrestle in college. He won championships. He said, "I don't care what's probable. Through blood, sweat, and tears, I am unstoppable."

1. When does the reader find out why Anthony hopped?
   a. start of the first paragraph
   b. middle of the first paragraph
   c. start of the second paragraph
   d. middle of the second paragraph

2. What did Anthony mean when he said, "I am unstoppable"?
   a. He will succeed because he will never give up.
   b. He will probably succeed.
   c. He will never cry—no matter how difficult it gets.
   d. He will stop when others tell him he can't do it.

3. An *adage* is a wise or traditional saying. What adage best fits this text?
   a. No risk, no gain.
   b. Too many cooks spoil the broth.
   c. Where there is smoke, there is fire.
   d. Birds of a feather flock together.

4. Why did the coaches begin to pay attention to Anthony?
   a. They knew he would start winning.
   b. He was always striving to improve.
   c. He was bothering the best wrestler on the team.
   d. He asked them for help with his attitude.

Name: _____

The Engine That Couldn't

"I think I can, I think I can, I think I can," said the little blue engine when it came to the towering hill. It puffed, and it huffed, and it exerted all of its strength. Steam billowed from its engine vents. The smell of burning metal and an overheated engine began to fill the air.

"I think I can, I think I can, I think I can," said the little blue engine, refusing to quit. The little blue engine doubled his efforts, but alas, it was all in vain. He just couldn't.

"You have a great attitude and work ethic," said the passenger car, "but as the ballerina Misty Copeland says, you need more. A good work ethic is required, but you also need a strong support team around you." Then, the passenger car said to all her passengers, "What are you waiting for? You should have volunteered already! Get off and start pushing! There's no such thing as a free lunch!"

1. When you *exert* yourself, you
   a. give up.   **b.** try hard.   **c.** refuse.   **d.** volunteer.

2. What does the saying "*There is no such thing as a free lunch*" mean?
   a. Lunch will not be served on the train until it is on the other side of the mountain.
   b. The engine can't work without being fed.
   c. There is always a cost. If you're not paying for it, someone else is.
   d. Lunches are free only to those who work hard or volunteer.

3. What lesson about success can be learned from this text?
   a. One's attitude is the most important thing.
   b. It requires doubling your efforts.
   c. One has to make other people help them.
   d. It takes a good work ethic and a support team.

4. Most likely, what is the subject of the next paragraph?
   a. how happy everyone was when the train got to the top of the hill
   b. how the train started down the hill before the passengers could get back on
   c. how the train went down the hill so fast that it crashed
   d. how the train couldn't get over the mountain, so everyone went hungry

Name: _____

House-Trained

"It took a great amount of effort, but my pet is completely house-trained," Lydia told Lincoln. "It was an arduous and difficult task. At times, I thought accomplishing it would be impossible, but now I am reaping the benefits. I'm getting in great shape, too."

"What did it take?" Lincoln asked, curiously. "What benefits are you reaping?"

"Oh, you don't know what lengths I had to go to!" Lydia said. "There were days when the furniture was toppled over! The noise it made when it fell was fearsome. Other days, clothes were strewn all over the house. Packages and papers were shredded. Food that was left out was completely demolished. One day, entire bags of animal crackers and sugar cookies were eaten!"

"Making a mess that large would take a lot of effort," Lincoln said.

"I know," Lydia said, "and I had to deal with it all on my own. My effort was rewarded though, because now my pet takes me outside at least three times a day. He even throws a ball that I get to retrieve over and over!"

1. What might happen if you didn't read the last paragraph carefully?
   a. You would not know that Lincoln is a cat.
   b. You would not know that papers were shredded.
   c. You would not know that clothes were strewn over the house.
   d. You would not know that a dog is telling the story.

2. Most likely, one reason Lydia is getting in shape is because
   a. she eats a lot of crackers and cookies.
   b. over and over she runs to pick up a ball.
   c. she is rewarded with treats.
   d. she had to deal with house training on her own.

3. When you *reap* something, you
   a. shred or destroy it.
   b. topple or knock it.
   c. gain or earn it.
   d. demolish or eat it.

4. An *adage* is a wise or traditional saying. What adage might Lydia like?
   a. A watched pot never boils.
   b. A fool and his money are soon parted.
   c. The squeaky wheel gets the grease.
   d. The pen is mightier than the sword.

Name: _____

A Voice

When Misty Copeland was thirteen years old, she was living in a shabby motel room. Her single mother slept in the only bed. Misty shared the floor with her five siblings. During that time, Misty attended a free ballet class at the local Boys and Girls Club. It changed her life.

Within three months of taking her first class, Misty was dancing *en pointe*. This is a style in which a dancer wears special pointe shoes. She then supports her entire body weight on the tips of her fully extended feet. Within a year, Misty was performing professionally. No other ballerina had ever started so late or progressed so quickly.

At one point, Misty was told her body wasn't right. She didn't look like traditional dancers. She was too curvy. Her muscles were too big. She wasn't rail-thin. It hurt to hear such things, but Misty persevered. She would not quit. Her work ethic paid off. She danced in major roles for a famous dance company. Then, on June 30, 2015, Misty was promoted. She became the company's principal ballerina. Misty was the first African-American woman to have risen to this position. Misty says that dancing gave her a voice. Her dancing tells people that dreams are possible.

1. This text is mainly about
   a. a ballerina who can sing.
   b. a dancer with a strong work ethic.
   c. what *en pointe* dancing is.
   d. Misty Copeland's family.

2. When someone keeps going and doesn't quit, he or she
   a. dreams.   **b.** changes.   **c.** extends.   **d.** perseveres.

3. An *adage* is a wise or traditional saying. What adage best fits this text?
   a. Don't judge a book by its cover.
   b. The early bird gets the worm.
   c. Curiosity killed the cat.
   d. You can't teach an old dog new tricks.

4. From the text, you can tell that most professional ballerinas
   a. perform in major roles after one year of classes.
   b. immediately dance *en pointe*.
   c. do not have siblings.
   d. start training at a very young age.

5. Why does Misty say that dancing gave her a voice?
   a. She talks to the audience about working hard when they come to see her dance.
   b. She dances in ballets that tell a story.
   c. She feels her dancing is a way of telling people their dreams can come true.
   d. She always dances when someone is singing.

Name: _____

Math Facts

"When does 11 plus 3 equal 2?" Molly asked her friend Ian. Ian told Molly that was an unsolvable problem. Molly said, "You're not thinking outside the box. When you add 3 hours to 11 o'clock, it equals 2 o'clock."

Ian said, "Two fathers and two sons sat down to eat eggs for breakfast. They ate exactly three eggs, and each person ate exactly one egg." When Molly objected that it wasn't possible for four people to eat three eggs and have one each, Ian told her that she wasn't going about solving the problem in the right way. "You're barking up the wrong tree," he said. Then he explained. "One of the fathers is also a grandfather. Therefore the other father is both a son and a father."

Molly said, "Let's do something together. Let's get a checkers board. Let's put a grain of rice on the first square. Now, let's double the amount on the next square. Let's double the amount every day until all the squares are filled."

"It's possible with pen and paper," Ian said, "but isn't possible with real rice because the amount is too big. The numbers will become astronomical sooner than you think."

1. If Ian asked Molly how she could make the number seven even, Molly would tell him
   - **a.** to remove the letter s.
   - **b.** to remove the letter v.
   - **c.** to remove the letter n.
   - **d.** to remove the letter e.

2. If something is *astronomical*, it is
   - **a.** on a square.
   - **b.** huge.
   - **c.** a puzzle.
   - **d.** easy.

3. What does the phrase *thinking outside the box* mean?
   - **a.** You are thinking while outside a box.
   - **b.** You are thinking differently or creatively.
   - **c.** You are thinking in the usual way.
   - **d.** You are thinking about playing with blocks.

4. There are 64 small squares on a checkerboard. By the 41st square, there would be over one trillion grains of rice. A trillion is
   - **a.** 100
   - **b.** 1,000
   - **c.** 1,000,000
   - **d.** 1,000,000,000,000

5. What adage or proverb might Molly like?
   - **a.** Two heads are better than one.
   - **b.** Too many cooks spoil the broth.
   - **c.** Curiosity killed the cat.
   - **d.** The early bird gets the worm.

Name: _____

Write On!

In the texts "The Wrestler," "House-Trained," "A Voice," and "Math Facts," there is a question about a proverb or adage. Choose two of these proverbs or adages and explain why they apply to each of the stories. Defend your answer by using specific examples from each text.

_____

_____

_____

_____

_____

_____

_____

_____

_____

_____

_____

_____

_____

_____

_____

_____

_____

_____

_____

_____

Name: _____

Chain-Mail Suit

Valerie Taylor put on a chain-mail suit. Chain mail is a type of armor made of small metal rings linked together to form a mesh. Valerie was not dressing up as a knight from medieval times. She was not preparing to fight. She was going swimming. The suit was very heavy, and it made swimming very difficult. Why would Valerie wear it?

Valerie and her husband made documentaries. They wanted to educate people about sharks. To do that, they wanted to film sharks close-up. They filmed sharks from inside a cage, but they wanted to get even closer.

The Taylors had the chain-mail suit made. Then, they had to test it out. Before Valerie got into the water, she did something to the suit. She put pieces of fish in the sleeves. When a blue shark tried to take a bite out of her arm, the cameras were rolling!

1. What movie is most likely a documentary?
   a. *Panda Bear Goes to Mars*
   b. *Termites of the African Plains*
   c. *Kangaroo and the Monster*
   d. *Ant's Antarctic Adventure*

2. What adjective fits with how the Taylors most likely felt about their suit?
   a. unsure   b. silly   c. anxious   d. confident

3. What type of shark tried to bite Valerie's arm?
   a. a sand shark
   b. a great white shark
   c. a lemon shark
   d. a blue shark

4. This text is mainly about
   a. what chain mail is.
   b. a couple who filmed sharks close-up.
   c. how to educate people.
   d. getting bitten by a shark.

Name: _____

Shark Safe

Sam said, "People have long been trying to find ways to protect themselves from shark attacks. They have tried shark cages, repellents that smell bad, and nets. I've invented something for people who are shipwrecked.

"It's an inflatable bag that you fill with sea water. It stays afloat because the top is an orange inflatable ring. The orange makes it easier for search parties to spot you. Sharks find their victims by sniffing blood or body waste. This bag defends against a shark's acute and keen sense of smell. Nothing gets out of the bag, so there is nothing to detect. Sharks are also attracted to flailing limbs. People are self-contained in my bag, so there are no thrashing limbs. They won't be able to detect any electrical signals from your body, either."

"Wow!" Sam's friend Louis said. "That sounds like a fantastic invention."

Sam nodded in agreement before asking, "Want to be the first to try it?"

1. What is not mentioned as something that attracts sharks?
   a. your blood
   b. your flailing limbs
   c. your voice
   d. your body waste

2. What might be a better title for this text?
   a. "A Fantastic and Successful Invention."
   b. "How People Stay Safe."
   c. "An Invention That Needs Testing."
   d. "How Sharks Detect People."

3. When something is *repelled*, it
   a. is driven away.
   b. is attracted.
   c. is drawn to something.
   d. is spotted.

4. Sam hopes that his invention helps
   a. people who are surfing.
   b. people who are scuba diving.
   c. people who are swimming at the beach.
   d. people who are shipwrecked.

Name: _____

Amazing Me!

I'm tired of everyone saying that the hammerhead shark is the strangest and most unique animal. I don't care that it has a head like a hammer with eyes on each end. I'm pretty amazing, too. In fact, I'm more than amazing. I'm stupendous! I'm an undercover wonder!

I can grow up to six and a half feet long, but still, you'd have a hard time spotting me. I'm an angel shark. I'm flat, and my mottled skin looks like sand. To complete my disguise, I bury my body in the sand by shuffling my fins. Only my eyes and spiracles poke out above the surface of the sand. When a fish comes near, I lunge forward, snap my jaws shut, and I feast!

Wondering what those spiracles are that I mentioned? Spiracles are special gill slits located just behind the eyes. Most sharks get oxygen by taking in water through their mouth. I take in water through my spiracles—it's less sandy and more likely to be free of silt. My spiracles supply oxygen directly to my eyes and brain when I'm undercover.

1. This text is written from
   a. the perspective of the angel shark.
   b. the perspective of a third person.
   c. the perspective of the hammerhead shark.
   d. the perspective of someone who doesn't like sharks.

2. How does an angel shark get its food?
   a. It swims after it and hunts it down.
   b. It waits for it and ambushes it.
   c. It takes it in through its spiracles.
   d. It spots it and then shuffles to it with its fins.

3. What adjective could be used to describe the narrator of this text?
   a. humble   b. modest   c. shy   d. proud

4. From the text, you can tell that the angel shark gets its oxygen from
   a. air.   b. sand.   c. water.   d. what it eats.

Name: _____

Unknown

On November 15, 1976, a ship was cruising off the Hawaiian island of Oahu. The ship deployed two sea anchors. A sea anchor is like a large parachute. It does not tether a boat to the seabed. When it is deployed, it drags along in the ocean while the ship is in motion. It slows the ship down.

When the sea anchors were hauled up, something dead was entangled in it. It was huge. It was over fourteen and a half feet long. It weighed over a thousand pounds. It had a mouth that was over three feet wide. It was an unknown shark! How could such a large creature stay hidden and undiscovered for so many years?

Today, this colossal shark is known as the megamouth shark. Less than 100 have ever been seen. One scientist may have the explanation. Megamouths are filter feeders. They feed on krill—tiny, shrimplike creatures. The scientist swam with and tagged a megamouth. The scientist discovered that the shark swam 450 to 500 feet below the surface feeding on krill. At night, when the krill ascended to 39 to 46 feet below the surface, so did the megamouth shark. The scientist hypothesized that the shark was seldom seen because it only swam near the surface during the dark hours of the night.

1. How is a sea anchor different from a regular ship's anchor?
   a. The sea anchor is used less often.
   b. The sea anchor weighs more than a thousand pounds.
   c. The sea anchor is not dropped to the ocean floor.
   d. The sea anchor floats in the sky.

2. At what depth are you most likely to spot a megamouth shark?
   a. at the surface
   b. 10 feet below the surface
   c. 475 feet below the surface
   d. 1,000 feet below the surface

3. Most likely, why was the scientist at little risk of being bitten by the megamouth shark?
   a. The shark's mouth was only three feet wide.
   b. The shark was a filter feeder and only ate tiny animals.
   c. The scientist remained in a shark cage for protection.
   d. The scientist swam with a chain-mail suit on.

4. When something is *huge*, it is
   a. colossal.
   b. deployed.
   c. hypothesized.
   d. tagged.

5. When the megamouth *ascended*, it
   a. went up towards the surface.
   b. went after the sun rose.
   c. went deeper below the surface.
   d. went before the sunset.

Name: _____

Stuffed Animal

Kim said, "Mom, have you ever heard of the planet Zacto?" Kim's mother responded that there was no planet Zacto. When she asked why Kim was asking, Kim said, "My friend Lllllt says he came from there. Want to make his acquaintance?"

When Kim's mother saw what Kim was holding, she burst out laughing. "That is the strangest stuffed animal I've ever seen! Wherever did you find it?"

"I didn't find him," Kim explained. "Lllllt found me. Their space probes just discovered Earth, so he came down to investigate."

Later than evening, Kim's mom was talking to Kim's older sister Donna. "Your little sister is something else," she said. "She found this tiny stuffed animal. It fits in the palm of her hand. She tried to convince me that it was an extraterrestrial. I couldn't be persuaded, of course, because aliens don't exist. I told her that if there truly was a planet Zacto, our astronomers would have found it already."

"That is exactly what our astronomers said about this planet. That's why I was sent to investigate." Kim's mother and sister didn't know who had spoken until they saw Lllllt fly through the air and land calmly on Donna's head.

1. What can the reader tell about extraterrestrials from this text?
   a. They can all fly.
   b. They all send out space probes.
   c. They are all small.
   d. They do not come from Earth.

2. What is Kim's mother assuming in the text?
   a. Astronomers have discovered every planet.
   b. Kim read a book about space probes.
   c. When Donna was little, she believed in aliens.
   d. Kim enjoys playing with stuffed animals more than dolls.

3. When you are *convinced*, you are
   a. investigated.   b. strange.   c. persuaded.   d. discovered.

4. This text is mainly about
   a. strange stuffed animals.
   b. a girl's family not believing what she said.
   c. what astronomers do.
   d. an extraterrestrial visit.

5. Most likely, what is the size of Lllllt?
   a. one foot tall, six feet wide
   b. two inches tall, two inches wide
   c. four feet tall, seven inches wide
   d. six inches tall, five feet wide

Name: _____

Write On!

Imagine that you are a megamouth shark. Use information from the stories to compare yourself to an angel shark. Make sure that you describe both differences and similarities. Then, write a paragraph in which you describe either an interaction with Sam's invention or with a scuba diver in a chain-mail suit. Should you swim away, or should you move in closer to explore? Are you scared? Nervous? Excited? Explain what you are feeling, what actions you take, and why. Remember, you are writing in the first-person perspective, so be sure to use the word *I*.

_____

_____

_____

_____

_____

_____

_____

_____

_____

_____

_____

_____

_____

_____

_____

_____

_____

_____

_____

_____

Name: _____

Fire and Water

Bright orange flames lit up the sky. Approximately 60 acres of land—the equivalent of 45 football fields—were being burned every minute! Firefighters raced to the flames. They came to fight the fire, but they did not have hoses. The only water they had was in the canteens they carried. How could the firefighters fight the fire? How could they extinguish the flames?

The firefighters used tools to make a firebreak. They used shovels, rakes, and chainsaws. They used Pulaskis, too. A Pulaski is a tool with a dual purpose. It can be used to chop wood or to dig in the soil.

A firebreak can measure anywhere from three to ten feet wide. The firefighters strip the land of all burnable material. They clear away branches, leaves, and grass. The firefighters contain the fire by making a firebreak all around it. The fire cannot cross the firebreak because it has nothing to burn. It has nothing to fuel it.

1. Most likely, the water in the canteens was
   a. for the firefighters to put on the flames.
   b. for the firefighters to use if they caught on fire.
   c. for the firefighters to drink.
   d. for the firefighters to wash their hands.

2. Most likely, the Pulaski's dual purpose makes it very valuable to a firefighter because
   a. it reduces the amount of weight they have to carry.
   b. it can be used to carry water.
   c. it increases the amount of time it takes for a firefighter to reach the flames.
   d. it can be used as fuel when needed.

3. When something is *extinguished*, it is
   a. burning.　　　　b. put out.　　　　c. lit.　　　　d. spreading.

4. Most likely, why don't city firefighters build firebreaks?
   a. Fires only burn 30 acres of land per minute in the city.
   b. It would be too hard to race upstairs carrying all the tools.
   c. It would be too difficult to clear the streets of fuel.
   d. They can't remove buildings, but they have water to spray on them.

Name: _____

Hot Work

When Mr. Chen came home, he was exhausted. "I've been lighting fires all day," he said. "The heat was fierce."

Mia listened incredulously. Lighting fires was not okay. How could Mr. Chen admit to such a thing? When Mr. Chen left the room, Mia turned to her friend Susan and asked, "Did I really just hear your father admit to lighting fires?"

"He does it all the time," Susan said. "He's a firefighter, you know."

Even more confused, Mia said, "I thought firefighters put out fires."

"Sometimes, forest firefighters use a special tool called a drip torch. It's a piece of equipment that shoots flames onto the ground. A backfire is a fire started on purpose to stop an advancing wildfire. The backfire burns all the fuel in front of it, and when the advancing fire meets the backfire, they both go out because there is nothing for them to burn."

1. This text is mainly about
   a. what two friends did together.
   b. a girl who learns about backfires.
   c. why Mr. Chen felt fierce.
   d. what happens when two fires meet.

2. What is the name of the tool used to start fires?
   a. a back torch   b. a drip torch   c. a back flame   d. a drip flame

3. When Mia was *incredulous*,
   a. she enjoyed listening.
   b. she knew exactly what Mr. Chen did.
   c. she did not believe what she was hearing.
   d. she was pleased with Mr. Chen's actions.

4. Most likely, the fuel the backfire used up
   a. was in the form of houses and lawns.
   b. was in the form of trees and buildings.
   c. was in the form of grass, leaves, and branches.
   d. was in the form of branches and schools.

Name: _____

Hungry, Hungry

I was so hungry that I felt weak. I wanted to eat, but nothing was available. All of the food was behind closed doors and in places I couldn't get to. Everyone was sleeping soundly, and it just made me mad. I could feel my blood begin to boil. How dare they sleep so soundly when I was so unhappy and miserable!

Furious, I ran to the bedroom. I made all the noise I could, and when I was ignored, I took hold of their blankets and I pulled them off! That's when they really started to yell and scream, but at least it spurred them to action! With me leading the way, they chased me downstairs! When they got to the kitchen, they wouldn't stop to feed me! Instead, they raced out the door! I kept pushing on their legs to get them to stop and turn around, but they didn't.

After the big red trucks came and water was sprayed everywhere, everyone wouldn't stop hugging me. I heard one man in a yellow suit say, "That dog is a real hero," but all I could think was, "This dog needs to be fed!"

1. Most likely, when the dog was pushing on the people's legs, the people
   a. knew the dog was hungry.
   b. were angry the dog had woken them up.
   c. believed the dog wanted to be hugged.
   d. thought the dog wanted them to go faster.

2. Most likely, where was all of the food?
   a. upstairs
   b. with the blankets
   c. in a cupboard
   d. on the red truck

3. When someone is *urged* or *encouraged* to do something, he or she is
   a. boiled.   b. miserable.   c. available.   d. spurred.

4. When does the reader find out that a dog is narrating the text?
   a. after a firefighter is heard saying something
   b. before the people were woken up
   c. when the dog is being chased
   d. when it gets hot enough for blood to boil

Name: _____

Last Resort

In 2016, six members of the Navajo Hotshot firefighter crew had no choice. They had to deploy their emergency shelters. This was their last resort. They had no other option.

The firefighters had been working on the last uncontrolled area of a large fire. There was a sudden change in how the fire was behaving. The firefighters could not get away fast enough. They were at risk of being engulfed in flames.

The emergency shelters are made of aluminum and silica. They can reflect 95 percent of the radiant heat of the flames. They are lightweight and can be quickly deployed. The firefighters did what they were trained to do. They threw away their packs. They brought only a liter of water and their radios under their shelters. They positioned themselves face down on the ground, grabbing the fiberglass handles. They sang, hummed, or yelled. This was to keep their minds off the pain and to keep up hope. They also had to paw at the ground beneath their mouths. This was so that they could try to bury their noses in the cooler air below. All six firefighters survived. When the ground was cool enough for them to walk on, they were able to rejoin the rest of their team.

1. From the text, you can tell that the emergency shelter
   a. is like a tent with a door.
   b. takes at least six minutes to deploy.
   c. is like a blanket with handles.
   d. keeps out all the heat.

2. From the text, you can tell that
   a. air temperature is the same at all levels.
   b. cold air rises.
   c. hot air rises.
   d. hot air sinks.

3. From the text, you can infer that the firefighters
   a. had deployed emergency shelters while in training.
   b. had never deployed an emergency shelter before.
   c. did not usually carry emergency shelters with them.
   d. needed more training to deploy their shelters correctly.

4. When someone *comes to their last resort*,
   a. he or she has a choice.
   b. he or she has no other options.
   c. he or she can try one of two things.
   d. he or she must be trained.

5. Another title for this text could be
   a. "Uncontrolled Fires."
   b. "All About Heat."
   c. "2016 Emergency."
   d. "Shelter from Fire."

Name: _____

Test Time

Bo had two older siblings named Maribel and Ken. Maribel and Ken were fraternal twins, not identical. At dinner, Maribel and Ken asked to be excused early. They said they had to start preparing for their test. "They are such responsible students," Bo's mother said proudly.

Bo and his mother watched as Maribel and Ken got their backpacks and started filling them with books. When the backpacks were bulging at the seams, Maribel and Ken put them on and stepped on a scale. "We need a little bit more," Maribel said. Nodding, Ken pushed two more books into each bag.

"Ready!" Maribel said, and the twins rushed out the door. When they returned, about 45 minutes later, they were drenched in sweat. "I love preparing for this test!" Maribel said.

Their mother snapped, "Enough of this nonsense! You get ready for tests by opening your books—not carrying them!" That's when Ken told her that they were going to apply to be Hotshot firefighters. "Part of the test is carrying a 45-pound pack three miles in less than 45 minutes," he said. "We also have to do 40 sit-ups and 25 push-ups in two minutes. Then, we have 11 minutes to run one and a half miles."

1. What can the reader tell about Hotshot firefighters from reading the text?
   a. They have to be strong and fit.
   c. They have to be a certain weight.
   b. They have to be a certain height.
   d. They have to be a certain age.

2. From the text, you can tell that the twins' mother
   a. was afraid the backpacks would break.
   b. did not know what being responsible meant.
   c. wanted the twins to do their sit-ups first.
   d. thought that the twins were going to be tested on facts.

3. When something is *bulging*, it is
   a. tired and exhausted.
   c. ripped and dirty.
   b. angry and frustrated.
   d. swollen and extended.

4. What did Maribel want to see when she stepped onto the scale?
   a. her weight
   c. a number 45 pounds more than her weight
   b. the number 45
   d. a number 45 pounds less than her weight

5. This text is mainly about
   a. twins preparing for a physical examination.
   b. a mother who is upset with all her children.
   c. a boy who has siblings who are twins.
   d. Hotshot firefighters.

Name: _____

Write On!

Based on your prior knowledge, give a general definition of a firefighter. Then, explain how a Hotshot firefighter differs from other firefighters. Use the information from the texts to describe what kind of fires Hotshot firefighters might fight, how they train, and what equipment they use.

Finally, explain whether you would want this job, and why.

_____

_____

_____

_____

_____

_____

_____

_____

_____

_____

_____

_____

_____

_____

_____

_____

_____

_____

Name: _____

Bird Woman

As everyone stared, the woman moved toward the airplane. When she arrived, she bent and laced a string around the hem of her dress. She tied the string in front—the same way you would tie a shoe. Who was this woman, and why did she tie a string around the hem of her dress?

The woman's name was Elise Deroche, and she was born in Paris, France in 1886. Elise tied the string around the bottom of her dress right before hopping into a seat on the plane. The string was needed to keep Elise's dress from flying up. Elise took her pilot's license test on March 8, 1910. When she passed, she became the first woman in the world to earn a pilot's license.

Elise became known as "*la femme oiseau*" or "*the bird woman.*" She entered aviation contests. She won many races. She also flew her plane in exhibitions.

1. When did Elise get her license?
   a. about 5 years after she was born
   b. about 20 years after she was born
   c. about 35 years after she was born
   d. about 50 years after she was born

2. What makes Elise Deroche an important person in history?
   a. She was the first woman to earn a pilot's license.
   b. She tied a string around the hem of her dress.
   c. She entered aviation contests and won many of them.
   d. She flew her plane in exhibitions.

3. Most likely, Elise was wearing a dress before flying because
   a. she wanted to dress up.
   b. at that time, women only wore long dresses.
   c. she was flying the plane to a dance.
   d. she thought a dress made her look more like a bird.

4. Most likely, the words *la femme oiseau* are
   a. French.
   b. English.
   c. Mandarin.
   d. Arabic.

la femme

Name: _____

One Day

When Joy stepped on a rock, it was so painful that she almost cried out. Quickly, she bit down on her lip. Joy knew that complaining wouldn't do any good. They had to get to California, and the wagon was already overweight with all that had been packed into it. Every family member had to walk.

Joy looked up to take her mind off the pain, and that was when she saw an eagle seeming to float on the wind. "Ma," Joy said, "wouldn't it be great if, one day, people could fly?"

Joy's mother reprimanded her. She said, "Stop spouting nonsense. Why, you might as well say that one day, humans will walk on the moon. You might even say that one day, people will be able to talk to each other when they are thousands of miles apart. Shame on you for filling your head with such ridiculous thoughts."

1. Most likely, Joy was
    a. stronger than her mother.
    b. an orphan.
    c. barefoot.
    d. someone who didn't help with chores.

2. What do we use today that Joy's mother said that thinking about was ridiculous?
    a. the car   b. the television   c. the bicycle   d. the phone

3. This text is mainly about
    a. a girl's thoughts while walking.
    b. why people rode in wagon trains to California.
    c. a mother who thought her daughter complained too much.
    d. how inventions are made.

4. When you are *reprimanded*, you are
    a. teased.   b. embarrassed.   c. scolded.   d. imaginative.

Name: _____

A Greek Myth

Daedalus and Icarus were imprisoned. Daedalus had made a great labyrinth for King Minos of Crete. The king was pleased with the maze, but he didn't want Daedalus to ever reveal how someone could get out of it. For that reason, the king had locked up both Daedalus and his son Icarus.

Daedalus was not to be thwarted. Nothing was going to stop him from escaping. Daedalus made two pairs of wings. He made his wings by first constructing a wooden frame. Then, using wax, he covered the frames with feathers. Daedalus warned his son to not fly too high. He cautioned him that flying too close to the sun would cause the wax to melt.

Icarus loved flying. He had never experienced such a wonderful feeling before. Icarus was having so much fun that he forgot his father's warning. Icarus flew higher and higher. He soared so high that the wax on his wings melted, and all the feathers came loose. Tragically, Icarus fell into the sea and died.

1. The title fits this text because a myth
   a. is a traditional story.
   b. is a nonfiction story.
   c. is a true story about an event that happened in the past.
   d. is a true story about an amazing and clever builder.

2. What did Daedalus do first when he made his wings?
   a. melt wax
   b. attach feathers
   c. construct a wooden frame
   d. collect feathers

3. When someone is prevented or stopped from doing something, he or she is
   a. imprisoned.   b. thwarted.   c. warned.   d. cautioned.

4. Why is this myth a tragedy rather than a comedy?
   a. Daedalus made wings.
   b. Icarus enjoyed flying.
   c. Daedalus warned his son.
   d. Icarus dies.

Name: _____

Off Course

Bob Gauchie was a Canadian bush pilot. On February 3, 1967, he was flying solo when his plane ran out of fuel. Bob was forced to land on a remote northern lake. No radio contact was possible. Bob knew that the odds were against him.

Bob survived on little more than a box of frozen fish. He endured high winds and temperatures that dropped to 60 degrees below zero. Several times, wolves circled the plane. Bob worried about starving, freezing, and being eaten. He also worried about succumbing to madness. Bob knew pilots who had been driven mad by isolation. Bob had not seen or talked to another human being in 58 days. How much longer could he stay sane?

Everyone assumed that Bob was dead. Search parties had long gone home. On April 1, Bob prepared himself for the end. It just so happened that, on that day, another bush pilot was off course. The pilot's passenger spotted a glint of light from the ground. When the pilot landed on the frozen lake surface, he and his passenger approached cautiously. They weren't sure if the ragged human before them had lost his mind. Bob cheerfully greeted them with a smile. Then, he asked them whether they had room for another passenger.

1. Most likely, when the bush pilot's passenger saw the glint, the bush pilot
   a. landed immediately.
   b. landed only after checking that his passenger hadn't succumbed to madness.
   c. got back on course before returning and landing.
   d. circled the area several times to investigate before landing.

2. What does the reader know about the temperature on the day that Bob was rescued?
   a. It was about 60 degrees below zero.
   b. It was still cold enough for the lake to be frozen.
   c. It was the warmest day of the year.
   d. It was stormy, which is what caused the second plane to land.

3. If someone has surrendered or yielded, he or she has
   a. succumbed.   b. become isolated.   c. assumed.   d. stayed sane.

4. What person is the most physically isolated?
   a. a person who is the only passenger on a bus going to the beach
   b. a person swimming laps in a city pool
   c. a person on a water slide in a water park
   d. a person on a small island in the middle of an ocean

5. This text can be summed up as
   a. a lesson about staying on course.   c. why people need to be kind to each other.
   b. the dangers of being a bush pilot.   d. a lucky survival tale.

Name: _____

Fast Flyer

"I wish I could fly," Niko said to his friend Wally. "I'd fly faster than anybody else."

Wally was the kind of friend who said things like, "*Can't* never did anything." Wally immediately began thinking about how Niko could fly. "You have to get a pilot's license," Wally said. "Your license type depends on what type of plane you want to fly. Single-engine plane licenses have different requirements than commercial jet licenses. You'll want a license that allows you to fly with instruments. You have to know how to use instruments if you're going to be flying at night or in an area with no landmarks."

Niko said, "That's too much work! I just wish I could fly without doing any preparation. I wish! I wish! I wish!"

The next day, Wally went to the corner where he met Niko so that they could walk to school together. Niko wasn't there, but Wally noticed something in the sky. Faster and faster, it plunged down. Wally saw that it was a peregrine falcon. Wally knew that peregrine falcons were the fastest birds in the world. When they dive, they can reach speeds of over 240 miles per hour! Wally couldn't wait to tell Niko what he had seen, but Niko never came.

1. Why do you think the author ended the text the way she did?
    a. to warn you to be careful about what you wish for
    b. to leave you thinking about Niko and his wish
    c. to teach you that if you want to fly, you need a license
    d. to make you afraid that Wally and Niko are no longer friends

2. A time that a pilot would most likely need to use instruments would be
    a. when flying over the Atlantic Ocean during a storm.
    b. when making a 20 minute flight in the morning.
    c. when circling a city park on a clear day.
    d. when taking a tourist to view a waterfall on an island.

3. When something *plunges*, it
    a. soars upward.   b. is prepared.   c. is required.   d. drops down suddenly.

4. This text is mainly about
    a. airplane pilot licenses and instruments.   c. a friend's wish and flying fast.
    b. the fastest bird and who saw it.   d. why one should never say *can't*.

5. When Wally said, "*Can't* never did anything," what did he mean?
    a. You always have to get ready and be prepared.
    b. He liked to do things that people thought he couldn't.
    c. He didn't think that Niko could ever fly a plane.
    d. If you give up before you start, you will never do anything.

Name: _____

Write On!

In the text "Fast Flyer," there is a line that says, "Wally was the kind of friend who said things like, '*Can't* never did anything.'"

Explain what Wally means. Then pick two of the following three texts: "Bird Woman," "A Greek Myth," "Off Course."

Tell why the main characters would agree with what Wally said. Support your answer by using information from the stories.

_____

_____

_____

_____

_____

_____

_____

_____

_____

_____

_____

_____

_____

_____

_____

_____

_____

_____

_____

Name: _____

Snail Bait

Mac Stone took off his shoes. He walked around in the waist-high water. All the while, he kept his eyes peeled for alligators. Why would anyone walk around barefoot in waist-high water where alligators lurked?

Stone was feeling for snails that Snail Kites feed on. Snails Kites are a kind of bird. They live in the Florida Everglades, and they feed exclusively on snails. Stone needed the snails so that he could bait the Snail Kites. When he found a snail, he put it on a platform and then waited for a Snail Kite to come down and snatch it so that he could take a photograph.

Usually, it is frowned upon to bait a bird for a photograph. This was a different case, as Stone was working with a biologist. The biologist was doing a study on the Snail Kite and its food supply. The photographs were needed for an article about the work that was being done.

1. Why was it okay for Stone to use snails as bait?
   a. He found the snails himself.
   b. The photographs that he took were for a scientific article.
   c. The alligators didn't eat the snails.
   d. Stone's photographs were for a nature photography contest.

2. When something is *lurking*, it is
   a. peeled.
   b. forgotten.
   c. lying in wait.
   d. sleeping soundly.

3. Where do the Snail Kites live?
   a. the Florida Everglades
   b. the Flower Gardens
   c. the French Waterways
   d. the Florida Shores

4. This text is mainly about
   a. photographs.
   b. a photographer preparing to take pictures.
   c. birds.
   d. what one kind of bird eats.

Name: _____

Gorilla Thoughts

Janelle didn't know what to do. The assignment was to make a comic book or a graphic novel. Janelle knew the difference. A comic book is read like a periodical. Comic books are produced weekly or monthly, and the story is continued. Graphic novels are read like books, and the tale ends on the last page. The problem was that Janelle was a terrible artist. Some people say that they have a hard time drawing circles. Janelle couldn't even draw a square!

"I wish I were a gorilla!" Janelle thought to herself in frustration. "Then I'd never have to go to school." The thought of the gorilla made a lightbulb go off! A gorilla's nose print is like a person's fingerprint. No one else has the same print. Janelle could make all her figures by using her thumbprint and fingerprints! It would be as easy as pie to draw eyes and a mouth on the prints and then add stick legs and feet.

1. From the text, you can tell that
    a. a gorilla can be indentified by its nose print.
    b. most gorillas have the same nose print.
    c. gorillas that have the same mother have the same nose print.
    d. gorillas do not have fingerprints.

2. A comic book would
    a. most likely be about new and different characters every week.
    b. most likely finish the story.
    c. most likely end like a graphic novel.
    d. most likely end with "to be continued."

3. This text presents
    a. a problem only.
    b. a problem and a solution.
    c. two problems.
    d. two problems and two solutions.

4. When it says in the text that *a lightbulb goes off,* it means
    a. that a lightbulb went off.
    b. that the room became light.
    c. that Janelle got an idea.
    d. that Janelle couldn't see what she was drawing.

Name: _____

Mother Goose

The goslings quacked for their "mother." They followed her everywhere, inside and outside. Their mother was good to them. She was there when they hatched. She always made sure that they had plenty of food, and she always kept them safe. Their mother was a good mother, but she wasn't like other mother geese. Their mother had two feet—like they did, but their mother had arms instead of wings.

Konrad Lorenz is a famous scientist. He has been called the "father of ethology." Ethology is the study of animal behavior. Lorenz said that many animals imprint on the first moving thing they see. When an animal imprints on something, it comes to recognize another animal, person, or thing as a parent or other object of trust.

Lorenz split a large clutch of goose eggs into two groups. Half was hatched by the mother goose. The other half was put into an incubator. When they hatched, the first thing they saw was Lorenz. Later, Lorenz put all the goslings under a box. He lifted the box. The goslings that saw the mother goose first went to her. The goslings that saw Lorenz first went to him. He had become their foster mother.

1. This text is mainly about
    a. goslings that were raised under a box.
    b. learning to trust your mother.
    c. a scientist who was both a "father" and a "mother."
    d. a science experiment.

2. Most likely, if some of the goslings had seen a cat first,
    a. they would follow the cat.
    b. they would be afraid that the cat would eat them.
    c. they would never learn how to swim.
    d. they would immediately start chasing mice.

3. All of the eggs that are inside a mother goose's nest are called
    a. a gosling.   b. an imprint.   c. a clutch.   d. an incubator.

4. An ethologist would most likely study
    a. what muscles an elephant uses to move its trunk.
    b. how otters learn to crack open clams.
    c. what feathers allow an owl to fly so quietly.
    d. how long whales live.

Name: _____

The Audition

Who would get the part? The first part of the audition was a simple test. If you didn't pass it, you would be eliminated. There would be no second chances. What was the first test? All it involved was walking by barking dogs. Any type of reaction would deem one not fit for the job. In order to pass, Miley had to ignore the commotion and remain silent and composed. Miley passed. Who was Miley, and what job was she applying for?

Miley is a husky-mix domestic dog. The San Diego Zoo had a wild, high-strung male cheetah. His name was Bakka. The zoo needed a companion for Bakka to help him relax and be less anxious. With her friendly and easy-going demeanor, Miley was a great candidate for the job.

After Miley passed the first test, she was kept in an enclosure right next to Bakka's. As the animals become more comfortable with each other, they were allowed physical contact when both were on leashes. At one point, when Miley was not on her leash, she took Bakka's leash and took him for a walk! Of course, Miley got the job!

1. What might a person audition for?
   a. a piece of bread
   b. a musical instrument
   c. a dream
   d. a part in a play

2. The author waited for the reader to find out who Miley was and what she was auditioning for so that you would
   a. worry that she would be eaten by a wild animal.
   b. be more interested in what job she was applying for.
   c. know that Miley was unable to bark.
   d. become anxious that Miley wouldn't pass the test.

3. From the text, you can tell that wild animals are
   a. not domestic.
   b. not anxious.
   c. not high-strung.
   d. not composed.

4. Why was Miley a great candidate for the job?
   a. She was a husky-mix.
   b. She didn't like wearing a collar.
   c. She barked a lot.
   d. She had a friendly demeanor.

5. The best title for this text is
   a. "Jobs at the San Diego Zoo."
   b. "Two Unlikely Friends."
   c. "All About Cheetahs."
   d. "Walking with and Without Leashes."

Name: _____

Jake's Friend

"I have a new friend," Jake announced. "He's really smart. When he wanted a drink of water, I filled the sink with water for him. Then he grabbed a leaf, crumpled it up by chewing on it, and then stuck it in the water. Then, he squeezed the water from the crumpled leaf into his mouth. He got seven or eight times more water that way than by dipping his fingers into the water."

Jake's brother Daniel said, "Why didn't your friend just use a glass?"

"Because," said Jake as he grabbed a bunch of bananas, "he's a chimpanzee. Chimpanzees can make simple tools."

"Oh," said Daniel nodding, "you've got another imaginary friend. Jake, don't you think you're getting too old for imaginary friends? Hey, where do you think you're going with all those bananas?"

"My friend is ravenous," Jake said. "He's really hungry because he hasn't been fed since early yesterday morning. I'm going to hold him as he eats because chimpanzees are like people. They are social animals and need to be cared for and nurtured."

When Daniel got to school, his friend Caleb asked him if he had seen a baby chimpanzee. "It escaped from the zoo early yesterday morning," Caleb said.

1. If you're feeling *ravenous*,
   a. you're really excited.
   b. you're really hungry.
   c. you're really scared.
   d. you're really imaginative.

2. From the text, you can tell that social animals
   a. live mostly on their own.
   b. only eat bananas.
   c. can all make simple tools.
   d. need to be with others and nurtured.

3. Most likely, what is the author hoping you'll wonder at the end of the text?
   a. what the name is of the chimpanzee that escaped
   b. how many other kinds of animals can make tools
   c. why the chimpanzee was able to escape from the zoo
   d. if Daniel is wrong about Jake's new friend being imaginary

4. What is one sure reason Daniel thinks Jake's friend is imaginary?
   a. Jake has had imaginary friends before.
   b. Jake is only three years old.
   c. Jake doesn't like bananas.
   d. Jake talks to his stuffed animals.

5. Using a simple tool, how much more water can a chimpanzee get than if it only used its fingers?
   a. five or six times more
   b. six or seven times more
   c. seven or eight times more
   d. eight or nine times more

Name: _____

Write On!

Use the following panels in order to create a comic strip about one of the texts in this unit. You may add information if necessary, but the overall story should remain the same. With your teacher's permission, you may use an inkpad to create thumbprint characters like the ones in "Gorilla Thoughts."

If your comic strip is not finished, write *"to be continued"* in the last panel.

Name: _____

Lost

Most likely, you have, at some point, lost a favorite toy or shirt. Objects are easy to forget. Can you imagine forgetting something that is worth four million dollars?

The high-priced article was a Stradivarius violin. It was left in the back seat of a taxi. Philippe Quint was a concert violinist. He had performed in Dallas, Texas. He was returning home to Manhattan, New York. He forgot the violin in the cab that drove him home from the airport. Quint was frantic. The violin wasn't even his! It had been lent to him!

Quint contacted the police immediately. His panic did not lessen until several hours later when the police called him. They told him that they knew where the violin was. It was at the taxi station. It had been turned in by the cab driver. The taxi driver's name was Mohammed Khalil. Khalil said, "Anybody out here would have done the same thing."

1. What do you know about the missing violin?
    a. It did not belong to Quint.
    b. It was worth five million dollars.
    c. It had been left in the front seat of a taxi.
    d. It was found by the cab driver in Texas.

2. When a person is *frantic*, he or she is
    a. honest and very truthful.
    b. panicked and wildly upset.
    c. forgetful and very scatterbrained.
    d. scared and wildly frightened.

3. One reason Quint may have forgotten the violin was that he was
    a. busy thinking about the concert he was going to perform.
    b. worried he might be late to the concert hall.
    c. tired after traveling and he just wanted to be home.
    d. busy looking at all the Dallas scenery.

4. This text is mainly about
    a. why violins are expensive.
    b. how many objects people forget.
    c. the day of a taxi driver.
    d. a musical instrument that was returned.

Name: _____

Forgotten

Sharon was a renowned horn player. She was famous for her ability to coax soft melodious notes from hard metal. By special request, Sharon was going to play for the queen. Sharon was excited, but she was also nervous.

Sharon went early to the concert hall. It was then that she realized that she had left her instrument at home! In a frenzied panic, Sharon called a taxi. She bit her fingernails all through the ride. At every red light, she felt her heart race. When she finally made it back to the concert hall, she was a nervous wreck. The other orchestra members were already seated and warmed up. Sharon felt sweat trickling down her back as she sat down.

The intermission was after Sharon's solo. "Why so tense?" asked the second-chair horn player. "You were fantastic." Sharon explained her near disaster. "I have an extra horn in my locker," the man said casually. "You could have used that."

1. A better title for this text might be
   a. "Musical Notes."
   b. "Orchestra Chairs."
   c. "The Queen Who Likes Horns."
   d. "Near Disaster."

2. In orchestras, musicians that play the same instruments are ranked. Most likely, Sharon is the
   a. first-chair horn player.
   b. second-chair horn player.
   c. third-chair horn player.
   d. fourth-chair horn player.

3. When did Sharon feel her heart race?
   a. when she played her solo
   b. all through the car ride
   c. when she realized her horn was at home
   d. at every red light

4. When a person is *renowned*, he or she is
   a. famous.   **b.** late.   **c.** forgetful.   **d.** skilled.

Name: _____

Break a Leg

A musician is about to perform. An actor is about to go on stage. One would think that this is the time to reassure the nervous performer. One should say something kind. Perhaps one should say, "Good luck!" Perhaps one should say, "Hope you have a great show." One could even say, "You're going to impress them!" or "You're more than ready." Instead, the tradition is for one to say something mean. It is to say something cruel. The tradition is to say, "Break a leg."

This expression came about because of a superstition. A superstition is an unfounded belief. It is not true. It is when one falsely believes that seeing or doing something causes something else to happen. An old superstition among musical or theatrical performers is that wishing a person "good luck" is actually considered bad luck. One should never reassure the person by telling them something nice. One should not say it will all go well. Instead, to wish one a successful show, one should wish something bad upon them. One should tell them to break a leg!

1. Another title for this text might be
    a. "Rules for Bringing Good Luck."
    b. "How to Make People Feel Better."
    c. "A Superstition Among Performers."
    d. "When a Superstition Began."

2. What fits the definition of a superstition?
    a. feeling happy when you see a yellow flower
    b. enjoying getting wet when it rains
    c. believing that seeing a black cat is bad luck
    d. knowing if you eat too much you will feel sick

3. Why shouldn't someone say, "You're going to be the star of the show!" to an actor or a musician?
    a. It is the same as telling them to do poorly.
    b. It makes the performer feel the other people aren't important.
    c. It is the same as telling the performer they should go high in the sky.
    d. It makes the performer worry that it will be dark soon.

4. A *tradition* is
    a. a cruel and mean action.
    b. a habit or a custom.
    c. a concert or a performance.
    d. a thing that is only done once.

Name: _____

Instrument Crafters

Antonio Stradivari was from Italy. He made about 1,000 violins. He built them in the late 1600s and 1700s. There are only about 650 left. Many musicians believe that no other violin can match a Stradivari violin. Nothing can equal their quality and sound. One reason is the wood Stradivari used. It is believed that temperatures were cooler from the 1200s to the mid-1800s. The cooler temperatures led to a denser or thicker tree bark. This, in turn, led to a wood that offered a superior sound.

The didgeridoo is another instrument. It is from Australia. It is not a string instrument like the violin. It is a wind instrument. One blows through it. The result is a droning sound. Who helps make a didgeridoo? It is something very small. It is not even human! It is a termite!

To make a didgeridoo, one uses a hollowed-out piece of wood. Many people feel that wood that has been hollowed out by termites produces a superior sound. The wood needs to come from a living tree. Dead hollowed out trees usually have cracks. They don't play as well. What's the best way of finding a suitable branch? Knock on it and listen! Cutting off the branch does not kill the tree.

1. One reason that Stradivari violins may be so expensive is because
   a. many people today know how to make violins.
   b. there are very few and no more are being made.
   c. you sound great when you play one even if you don't practice.
   d. since the 1700s, all violins have been made out of plastic.

2. From the text, you can tell that
   a. wood used for didgeridoos should be cracked.
   b. didgeridoos are a kind of string instrument.
   c. the best wood for a didgeridoo has a thick bark.
   d. hollow and solid branches sound different when knocked.

3. This text is mainly about
   a. expensive violins.
   b. two different kinds of instruments.
   c. an instrument made from a living tree.
   d. the places where two instruments come from.

4. Most likely, there
   a. will be more Stradivari violins than didgeridoos in 650 years.
   b. are the same number of didgeridoos today as Stradivari violins.
   c. are more didgeridoos today than Stradivari violins.
   d. are less didgeridoos today than Stradivari violins.

5. When something is *dense*, it is
   a. thick.   **b.** hollow.   **c.** superior.   **d.** suitable.

Name: _____

The Nightingale

The Nightingale is a fairy tale. It is very old. It was written by Hans Christian Andersen. It was first published in 1843. In the story, the emperor is told that the most beautiful thing in his empire is the sound of the nightingale. No one knows where the nightingale is except the kitchen maid. The maid takes the emperor to where the bird is singing. The bird agrees to go to court and sing for the emperor.

The bird sings and sings. The emperor is delighted. Then one day, the emperor is given a gift. It is a mechanical nightingale. It is covered in jewels. The emperor likes the bejeweled bird better. He forgets all about the real bird. No one notices when the real nightingale returns to the forest.

After some time, the emperor falls deathly ill. He wants to hear the sound of the nightingale, but the mechanical one has broken down. When the real nightingale learns of the emperor's condition, he flies to the emperor's bedside. He sings and sings. He sings so beautifully that Death allows the emperor to live.

"You can tell that is a really old and outdated story," Jenny said. She turned to her maid. She gave it an order. "Robot, add 'nightingale singing' to my playlist."

1. What best sums up this text?
   a. a very old fairy tale
   b. a very old fairy tale with an updated ending
   c. a very old story about mechanical inventions
   d. a very old tale about the importance of song

2. How do the two maids in the text differ?
   a. The first maid is mechanical.
   b. The first maid can sing like a nightingale.
   c. The second maid is mechanical.
   d. The second maid knows where a nightingale is.

3. Why does the real nightingale return to the emperor?
   a. He was ordered.   c. He wanted jewels.
   b. The maid begged him to.   d. He was kind.

4. Most likely, the author wants the reader to
   a. understand how only living things can be kind.
   b. think about how helpful robots are.
   c. learn that, if something is bejeweled, it is worth more.
   d. know that singing can't make you feel better.

5. Where does the nightingale live?
   a. by a stream   b. on a hill   c. in the country   d. in the forest

Name: _____

Write On!

Compare the mechanical nightingale to the violin that was left in the taxi. Give facts about how each one was made and what made each of the objects special. (You will be able to give more information about the violin than the bird.)

Then compare the real nightingale to the taxi driver. They have some obvious differences, but how are they similar? Explain your answer.

_____

_____

_____

_____

_____

_____

_____

_____

_____

_____

_____

_____

_____

_____

_____

_____

_____

_____

_____

_____

Tracking Sheet

Unit 1 (pages 6–11)		Unit 7 (pages 42–47)		Unit 13 (pages 78–83)	
What the Droop Means		Where's Who?		Chain-Mail Suit	
Desert Survival		Lifeforms		Shark Safe	
Surviving the Gorge		Diamante		Amazing Me!	
No Eyelids		Wrong Side Up?		Unknown	
The New Colony		The Forgery		Stuffed Animal	
Write On!		Write On!		Write On!	
Unit 2 (pages 12–17)		**Unit 8** (pages 48–53)		**Unit 14** (pages 84–89)	
Unforeseen Problem		Sailing Stones		Fire and Water	
A Brave Actor		World's Smallest		Hot Work	
Director's Choice		Hugs from Chile		Hungry, Hungry	
Snake's-Eye View		Two Caves		Last Resort	
Whale Watching		The Island		Test Time	
Write On!		Write On!		Write On!	
Unit 3 (pages 18–23)		**Unit 9** (pages 54–59)		**Unit 15** (pages 90–95)	
Just as Horrible		Riddle Sound		Bird Woman	
Deadly Spit		Making It Fun		One Day	
Six Questions		School Bus		A Greek Myth	
Not All!		Why the Chicken?		Off Course	
Frustrated and Weary!		50 Percent Chance		Fast Flyer	
Write On!		Write On!		Write On!	
Unit 4 (pages 24–29)		**Unit 10** (pages 60–65)		**Unit 16** (pages 96–101)	
Man-Eating Piranhas		Unfit to Drink		Snail Bait	
Nessie		The Important Guest		Gorilla Thoughts	
Optical Illusion		Rubbing Salt		Mother Goose	
Spaghetti Crop		All About Tears		The Audition	
More Than the News		The Magic Lamp		Jake's Friend	
Write On!		Write On!		Write On!	
Unit 5 (pages 30–35)		**Unit 11** (pages 66–71)		**Unit 17** (pages 102–107)	
Close but Unseen		Shipwrecked		Lost	
Yes and No		Stranded!		Forgotten	
Wanted		Castaway's Diary		Break a Leg	
The Green Wall		18 Years		Instrument Crafters	
Lance's First Day		Rescued!		The Nightingale	
Write On!		Write On!		Write On!	
Unit 6 (pages 36–41)		**Unit 12** (pages 72–77)			
Poured at Night		The Wrestler			
Walking on Water		The Engine That Couldn't			
A Play About Big and Bigger		House-Trained			
On a Pin		A Voice			
A Big Difference		Math Facts			
Write On!		Write On!			

Answer Key

Answer Key

Unit 1

What the Droop Means (page 6)

1. c   2. a   3. d   4. b

Desert Survival (page 7)

1. a   2. c   3. c   4. d

Surviving the Gorge (page 8)

1. c   2. b   3. a   4. a

No Eyelids (page 9)

1. d   2. a   3. b   4. c   5. b

The New Colony (page 10)

1. b   2. d   3. b   4. a   5. d

Unit 2

Unforeseen Problem (page 12)

1. d   2. d   3. b   4. a

A Brave Actor (page 13)

1. a   2. c   3. d   4. b

Director's Choice (page 14)

1. d   2. a   3. a   4. c

Snake's-Eye View (page 15)

1. b   2. d   3. c   4. c   5. d

Whale Watching (page 16)

1. c   2. a   3. c   4. d   5. b

Unit 3

Just as Horrible (page 18)

1. a   2. c   3. d   4. b

Deadly Spit (page 19)

1. c   2. a   3. a   4. c

Six Questions (page 20)

1. b   2. d   3. b   4. a

Not All! (page 21)

1. d   2. b   3. c   4. d   5. a

Frustrated and Weary! (page 22)

1. c   2. a   3. d   4. a   5. b

Unit 4

Man-Eating Piranhas (page 24)

1. d   2. a   3. c   4. a

Nessie (page 25)

1. b   2. d   3. c   4. b

Optical Illusion (page 26)

1. c   2. d   3. b   4. a

Spaghetti Crop (page 27)

1. a   2. c   3. a   4. d   5. c

More Than the News (page 28)

1. b   2. b   3. d   4. c   5. a

Unit 5

Close but Unseen (page 30)

1. b   2. c   3. d   4. a

Yes and No (page 31)

1. c   2. d   3. b   4. d

Wanted (page 32)

1. a   2. a   3. d   4. c

The Green Wall (page 33)

1. d   2. b   3. c   4. a   5. b

Lance's First Day (page 34)

1. b   2. c   3. d   4. b   5. c

Unit 6

Poured at Night (page 36)

1. b   2. b   3. d   4. d

Walking on Water (page 37)

1. a   2. c   3. d   4. b

A Play About Big and Bigger (page 38)

1. d   2. b   3. a   4. c

On a Pin (page 39)

1. c   2. d   3. c   4. a   5. b

A Big Difference (page 40)

1. d   2. d   3. b   4. c   5. a

Answer Key (cont.)

Unit 7

Where's Who? (page 42)

1. c   2. b   3. a   4. c

Lifeforms (page 43)

1. d   2. a   3. d   4. a

Diamante (page 44)

1. a   2. d   3. c   4. b

Wrong Side Up? (page 45)

1. b   2. d   3. b   4. c   5. c

The Forgery (page 46)

1. a   2. c   3. b   4. d   5. d

Unit 8

Sailing Stones (page 48)

1. b   2. d   3. a   4. c

World's Smallest (page 49)

1. c   2. b   3. d   4. b

Hugs from Chile (page 50)

1. a   2. c   3. b   4. a

Two Caves (page 51)

1. d   2. b   3. c   4. b   5. a

The Island (page 52)

1. d   2. d   3. a   4. a   5. c

Unit 9

Riddle Sound (page 54)

1. d   2. a   3. b   4. a

Making It Fun (page 55)

1. d   2. b   3. b   4. c

School Bus (page 56)

1. c   2. a   3. d   4. b

Why the Chicken? (page 57)

1. b   2. c   3. c   4. b   5. d

50 Percent Chance (page 58)

1. a   2. b   3. a   4. b   5. c

Unit 10

Unfit to Drink (page 60)

1. d   2. d   3. c   4. c

The Important Guest (page 61)

1. a   2. c   3. b   4. d

Rubbing Salt (page 62)

1. d   2. b   3. a   4. b

All About Tears (page 63)

1. b   2. a   3. c   4. d   5. d

The Magic Lamp (page 64)

1. c   2. c   3. d   4. a   5. a

Unit 11

Shipwrecked (page 66)

1. c   2. b   3. d   4. a

Stranded! (page 67)

1. b   2. a   3. b   4. d

Castaway's Diary (page 68)

1. a   2. c   3. c   4. b

18 Years (page 69)

1. d   2. d   3. a   4. c   5. c

Rescued! (page 70)

1. c   2. d   3. d   4. b   5. a

Unit 12

The Wrestler (page 72)

1. c   2. a   3. a   4. b

The Engine That Couldn't (page 73)

1. b   2. c   3. d   4. a

House-Trained (page 74)

1. d   2. b   3. c   4. c

A Voice (page 75)

1. b   2. d   3. a   4. d   5. c

Math Facts (page 76)

1. a   2. b   3. b   4. d   5. a

Answer Key (cont.)

Unit 13

Chain-Mail Suit (page 78)

1. b   2. d   3. d   4. b

Shark Safe (page 79)

1. c   2. c   3. a   4. d

Amazing Me! (page 80)

1. a   2. b   3. d   4. c

Unknown (page 81)

1. c   2. c   3. b   4. a   5. a

Stuffed Animal (page 82)

1. d   2. a   3. c   4. d   5. b

Unit 14

Fire and Water (page 84)

1. c   2. a   3. b   4. d

Hot Work (page 85)

1. b   2. b   3. c   4. c

Hungry, Hungry (page 86)

1. d   2. c   3. d   4. a

Last Resort (page 87)

1. c   2. c   3. a   4. b   5. d

Test Time (page 88)

1. a   2. d   3. d   4. c   5. a

Unit 15

Bird Woman (page 90)

1. b   2. a   3. b   4. a

One Day (page 91)

1. c   2. d   3. a   4. c

A Greek Myth (page 92)

1. a   2. c   3. b   4. d

Off Course (page 93)

1. d   2. b   3. a   4. d   5. d

Fast Flyer (page 94)

1. b   2. a   3. d   4. c   5. d

Unit 16

Snail Bait (page 96)

1. b   2. c   3. a   4. b

Gorilla Thoughts (page 97)

1. a   2. d   3. b   4. c

Mother Goose (page 98)

1. c   2. a   3. c   4. b

The Audition (page 99)

1. d   2. b   3. a   4. d   5. b

Jake's Friend (page 100)

1. b   2. d   3. d   4. a   5. c

Unit 17

Lost (page 102)

1. a   2. b   3. c   4. d

Forgotten (page 103)

1. d   2. a   3. d   4. a

Break a Leg (page 104)

1. c   2. c   3. a   4. b

Instrument Crafters (page 105)

1. b   2. d   3. b   4. c   5. a

The Nightingale (page 106)

1. b   2. c   3. d   4. a   5. d